- *in love with* -

Flying

- in love with -

Flying

Kenneth W. Ford

H Bar Press
Philadelphia, Pennsylvania
Wallingford, Vermont
2007

In Love With Flying
by Kenneth W. Ford

H Bar Press
729 Westview St. • Philadelphia, PA 19119
www.hbarpress.com

Printed in the U.S.A. (2nd Printing)

Book design and cover photo by Adam B. Ford

Body text is Iowan Old Style Roman, 11 point. Cover text
is Ex Ponto Regular. Cover: Harris Hill, Elmira, New York.
Back cover: Ken Ford next to L-19 tow plane, PGC Airport, Bucks
County, Pennsylvania, ~1992. Background image: FAA sectional
chart; Albuquerque

Illustrations by Cornelia J. Cesari

Chapter 1: Ercoupe; Chapter 2: Aeronca Champion "Champ";
Chapter 3: SPTVAR; Chapter 4: Rolladen-Schneider LS-4;
Chapter 5: Beechcraft Bonanza; Chapter 6: Airbus A300-600;
Chapter 7: Starduster; Chapter 8: L-19 (Cessna 305A);
Chapter 9: Cessna 172 Skyhawk; Chapter 10: Schweizer 1-26

Publisher's Cataloging-in-Publication Data

Ford, Kenneth William, 1926-

In love with flying / Kenneth W. Ford.

240 p. 22 cm.

ISBN 978-0-9794104-1-3 (paperback)

1. Air pilots—United States—Biography. 2. Private
flying. 3. Gliders (Aeronautics)—Piloting.

TL540.F67 2007

629.13'092—dc22   2007928027

*To all the pilots I have met and all the passengers
I have carried. You are one giant family.*

*And in memory of
Robert N. (Bob) Buck
1914 - 2007*

Contents

Foreword · ix

1 First Flight · 1

   Profile: Charles J. (Charlie) Boyd · · · · · · · · · · · 13

2 Becoming a Pilot · 25

   Profile: John Myers · 36

3 Soaring · 45

   Profile: Alcide (Al) Santilli · · · · · · · · · · · · · · · 58

4 The Landing · 68

   Profile: Antonio (Tony) Sabino · · · · · · · · · · · · 78

5 From A to B · 87

   Profile: Laszlo (Les) Horvath · · · · · · · · · · · · · 98

6 All of a Piece · 112

   Profile: Christine (Chris) Doig · · · · · · · · · · · · 125

7 All Kinds of Air, All Kinds of Flying · · · · · · · 137

   Profile: Carl Ray Smith · · · · · · · · · · · · · · · · · · 149

8 Buttoning Up and Getting Going · · · · · · · · · 161

   Profile: J. William (Bill) Bullock · · · · · · · · · · · 173

9 Helping Out · 182

   Profile: Gerald (Jerry) Hoogerwerf · · · · · · · · · 193

10 Making It · 205

   Afterword · 219

   Acknowledgements · 220

Foreword

What motivated this book? First of all, my fifty-year love affair with flying. Second, my admiration, often tinged with awe, for the many people I met along the way who gave up whatever more lucrative careers might have been out there to do what they most loved doing, which was to fly. Since what I flew were small airplanes and gliders, out of small airports and landing strips, the professional aviators I met were mostly not airline pilots or corporate pilots. They were airport operators, flight instructors, weather flyers, environmental flyers, glider pilots, tow pilots, or just pilots for hire. And quite a few of them loved fixing airplanes almost as much as flying them.

So this book is partly a memoir of my own life in the air and partly a set of profiles of some of those remarkable flyers whom I came to know over the years. On the ground I have been a physicist and a teacher, in the air an earnest amateur. There's no physics in this book, but I haven't been able to resist doing a little teaching—for instance, about old and new ways to navigate, the different kinds of lift available to glider pilots, and the hazards of box canyons.

If you're not a pilot but thinking of becoming one, whatever your age, you might enjoy this book. If you want to learn a little more about the lure of the sky that goes beyond anecdotes, scary or amusing, these pages might be for you. And if you're a fellow pilot, you might like to compare my experiences and observations with your own.

-1-

First Flight

There is something about New Mexico that beckons one aloft—endless skies, gorgeous mountains, mesas rising nearly vertically from the desert floor, cumulus clouds piled up like gobs of whipped cream (sometimes, when you fly through them, they feel more like potatoes not fully mashed).

That's where I got hooked on flying. It was 1953. I was 27. I had had only one previous flight in a small plane. A year earlier, a sixteen-year old boy with a pilot's license, the son of a security guard at the Princeton lab where I was working, invited me for a flight in a Piper Cub (Piper J-3, as it was officially called). I was entranced as he did spins (illegal with me aboard) and buzzed his girlfriend's house (also illegal). The seed was planted.

I had just earned a Ph.D. in physics at Princeton and was spending the summer at the atomic laboratory in Los Alamos. A couple of years earlier, I had been a junior member of the H-bomb design team there, and had then worked at a satellite lab of Los Alamos in Princeton. So I had saved a bit of money. For $1,700—most of my savings—I bought a new Plymouth in Trenton, New Jersey, and drove west in it. But once I got settled again in New Mexico, something clicked in my brain. I needed to fly.

In nearby Española I found a buyer for my lovely new Plymouth, and parted with it for, if I remember correctly, $1,600 (the loss was not greater because at that time new cars cost more in New Mexico than in New Jersey). Then I invested $200 in an old Chevrolet, and looked for an airplane. A Los Alamos pediatrician wanted to sell his little two-place Ercoupe in order to buy a fancier four-place Bonanza. We negotiated a price of $1,100. I had enough left over to pay an instructor to teach me to fly it.

I had to keep my airplane at the Santa Fe Airport, some forty miles from Los Alamos. At the time, no private flying was permitted from the Los Alamos airstrip. That airstrip, long, wide, and paved, was located atop a mesa at an elevation of 7,171 feet.* From aloft, it looks a bit like a giant aircraft carrier docked against the Jemez Mountains. The only planes that landed at Los

---

* This official elevation is for the highest point on the runway. Out west, where sloping runways are common, the difference between the high end and low end may be significant. Once, when gaining altitude after taking off from the airstrip at Eagle Nest, New Mexico, I glanced at my altimeter and noticed that I was well below the elevation where I had been when beginning the takeoff run.

Alamos at the time belonged to a New Mexico carrier called Carco (founder and owner Clark Carr, an Albuquerque pilot and businessman), plus the occasional government plane. Carco ferried people back and forth between Los Alamos and Albuquerque, sixty miles away (ninety miles by road), in small planes, four-seaters and six-seaters, some with one engine, some with two. That meant that, for me, the best part of any trip from Los Alamos to the east or west coast was the half hours spent at the beginning and end of the trip in a Carco plane. I always graciously let others board ahead of me so that I could take the remaining seat up front next to the pilot.

Carco pilots, some of them grizzled Old-West types—including Clark Carr himself—did what they could to propagate the myth that landing at Los Alamos, with its thin air, gusty winds, and up and down drafts, was far too tricky for an ordinary pilot. Actually, it was probably the Atomic Energy Commission's concern for security more than Mr. Carr's influence that kept private pilots at arm's length. Mr. Carr's exclusive contract persisted, with or without private pilots. Eventually, in 1960, the restricted zone over the town and neighboring canyons was reined in to cover only the laboratory areas, and private pilots began to use the airstrip. From my first flight out of Los Alamos in 1970, when I was living there, to my last, in 1995, when I was visiting, I logged some eighty landings (and takeoffs), flying several models of Cessna aircraft as well as a Stinson, a Beech Bonanza, a Mooney, and a Bellanca Viking. It was manageable. One small problem was that almost all landings had to be made to the west and all takeoffs to the east on the single strip, to assure that approaching and departing planes didn't fly over any lab buildings, and to take advantage of the west-to-east downslope of the runway. (Occasionally, in a roaring wind, takeoffs uphill or landing downhill were permitted.) In the late afternoon, landing at Los Alamos could be made interesting by having the bright southwestern sun full in your face. As one Carco pilot said to me after negotiating such a landing (as usual, I was riding in the co-pilot's seat), "I couldn't see the runway, so I had to feel for it."

The Santa Fe Airport was managed by Charlie Boyd. He sold gas, ferried business people around the state, flew missions for the United States Forest Service in his Piper Super Cub, taught student pilots how to fly—and may have cut the grass, too. His airport had one paved runway and a couple of grass runways at other angles, used when the wind favored them. The Santa Fe Airport later became the Old Santa Fe Airport after the city built a bigger and better one a few miles away. The new one had three paved runways, one of them long enough to accommodate commercial airliners. (There was a time in the 1960s when you could board a TWA or Frontier or Trans-Texas flight in Santa Fe. After that, you had to drive to Albuquerque to get on a long-distance flight.) Still later, the Old Santa Fe Airport became an industrial park and State Police Headquarters. You would be hard pressed now to find evidence that it was once an airport.

$\mathcal{M}$y first flight with Charlie in my Ercoupe occurred on July 3, 1953, and lasted half an hour. This made for the first entry in my log book, under the heading "Dual." Still sitting there on page 1 of the first of my seven log books is the signature C. J. Boyd and the notation C (for Certificate) 37769.*

The Ercoupe (usually pronounced AIR-coop) is a remarkable plane. Like most small planes at the time, it was built in a wave of airplane production right after World War II. More small planes were turned out in 1946-1947 than in all of the preceding years combined, and it's likely that the 1946 single-year production has never been matched since. It was a gigantic peak. (And, as you might guess, most of the companies engaged in making planes then are no longer in business.) The Ercoupe was, for its time, quite advanced. It had a metal skin of shiny aluminum (I say "had" although quite a few of them are still flying). Most others of the period—the Aeroncas, Taylorcraft, and Pipers—had skeletons of steel rods covered with stretched fabric (many of those are still flying, too). The Ercoupe had a tricycle landing gear, meaning that it had two main wheels toward the middle of the plane and a nose wheel up front. On the ground, it sat more or less level. The competition had mostly "conventional" landing gear—two wheels further forward and a small tail wheel, or sometimes only a metal tail skid, at the back. Such a plane sits on the ground with its nose angling up toward the sky. This arrangement was the norm in the 1930s—thus the term

* See page 222

"conventional"—but the tricycle gear has long since become the norm. The famous old DC-3, a workhorse of early airlines and of the military in the 1940s (and still flying, too!) had a conventional landing gear. Every airliner since has had tricycle gear.

And the Ercoupe was fast. With an engine of 75 horsepower (the earliest models had 65, later ones 85 horsepower), it could cruise at 100 miles per hour, thus easily passing automobile traffic below (actually, I have encountered headwinds so strong that freeway traffic on the ground was passing me). The fabric-covered "tail draggers," as they were called, with similar engines, putted along more in the range of 80 to 90 miles per hour. The Ercoupe was designed—and eventually manufactured and sold—by a brilliant and little appreciated engineer named Fred Weick.* Back in the early 1930s he was an expert on propeller design and on the design of cowlings, the metal covers over engines. In the late 1930s he conceived the Ercoupe and had the savvy to make it as well as design it. His factory was located in Riverdale, Maryland, not far from the University of Maryland campus in College Park. Much later, when I was involved in selecting a site for a new physics building at that very place, I helped myself to a piece of the black pavement of the airstrip from which all the new Ercoupes had flown away from the factory, before that strip, on behalf of commercial development, was

---

* Fred Weick tells his story with co-author James R. Hanson in *From the Ground Up: The Autobiography of an Aeronautical Engineer* (Washington, D.C.: Smithsonian Institution Press, 1988).

destroyed. That piece of runway, lacquered to keep it from blackening everything it touches, sits now on my desk as a valued paperweight. A colleague who was with me in 1992 when I asked that the car we were riding in stop so that I could get out and collect my piece of the runway said, "Ken, you're weird." He didn't appreciate the romance of the air.

When learning to fly, the student pilot sits in the pilot's seat but is not the "pilot in command." Charlie had that honor. The rules of the sky are not unlike those of the sea; there is always a captain in command. Most of the two-place planes of the time—the "tail draggers"—had tandem seating. The student sat in front where the instruments and more of the outdoors were visible. Sitting behind, with at least a partial set of duplicate instruments in view, and ready to shout as needed, was the instructor. The Ercoupe, again ahead of its time, had side-by-side seating. The student sat on the left, the instructor on the right. Both types of airplanes had linked controls available so that the instructor could take over if necessary. Most tail draggers had a "stick" for each pilot, a vertical rod hinged at floor level between the pilot's legs. Moving the stick fore and aft controlled the elevator on the tail to lower and raise the nose. Moving the stick left and right controlled the ailerons on the wings to bank the wings left or right. In the Ercoupe, and in many later planes, a wheel attached to a horizontal rod performed the same functions as a stick. The wheel could be pushed in or pulled out to control the elevator, and could be turned left or right to control the ailerons.

The tail draggers—and, in fact, every other airplane ever built, so far as I know, from Piper Cubs to Boeing 747s, *except* the Ercoupe—also had rudder pedals, linked together so that if the left pedal moved forward, the right pedal moved back. Rudder pedals control the rudder on the tail. Pushing the left pedal makes the rudder swing to the left, causing the flow of air past it to push the tail to the right, which in turn swings the nose to the left. Pushing the right pedal does the opposite. So, to go left, push left; to go right, push right. For a short time, this caused me a problem when I was introduced later that year to flying the Aeronca Champ, a classic taildragger. At first I couldn't get out of my head my childhood experience with a kiddie car. In the kiddie car, the child's feet rest on the two ends of a front axle that can swing. The rule is: To go left, push with the right foot; to go right, push with the left foot—opposite to the rule in the airplane. This short-term problem was postponed for me because of the Ercoupe's lack of rudder pedals. This doesn't mean the Ercoupe had no rudder. It did. Its rudder control was interconnected with the aileron control so that the wheel performed three functions, not two. This was an innovation that didn't catch on.

Actually, the main function of a rudder is not to turn the plane. Turning is accomplished by banking, thus controlled mainly by the ailerons. What the rudder does is keep the controls "coordinated," so that the direction in which the plane is moving through the air and the direction in which it is pointing are the same. Rudder pressure must be applied when entering and leaving a turn to keep this coordination. The problem is that there are times when the pilot doesn't *want* the controls to be coordinated. This occurs when landing in a cross wind. In coordinated flight (mandated in an Ercoupe), the nose of the plane is pointing in the direction the plane is moving relative to the air, but not necessarily relative to the ground. Relative to the ground, the airplane is "crabbing," with its nose tilted somewhat into the wind as it moves above the runway. So when an Ercoupe lands in a crosswind, it must execute a quick fouetté just after touching down, swinging its nose from whatever angle it had relative to the runway to alignment with the runway. With separate rudder control, the pilot can deliberately fly uncoordinated in the final approach to the landing (with crossed controls, as it's called). Then the airplane, just before landing, has its upwind wing lowered a bit and its nose pointing along the runway. Now it's crabbing relative to the air but not relative to the ground. (Years later, at La Guardia Airport, while I was waiting my turn to take off, I watched a parade of commercial jets landing in a cross wind. Their pilots maintained coordinated flight, with the planes' noses not perfectly aligned with the runway, until just before touchdown. At the last moment, they kicked—perhaps literally—their planes into uncoordinated flight, pulling the nose around to point down the runway. The passengers got a smooth ride and a relatively gentle touchdown. No fouetté required.)

O nce during my five weeks as a student pilot in Santa Fe, Charlie Boyd invited me to accompany him on a Forest Service mission over the Jemez mountains. I sat in the back of his Super Cub. (This plane is "super" in that it is a little larger than the old original Cub and a good deal more powerful. Like the original, it has fore-and-aft tandem seating and is a stick-and-rudder plane.) Charlie's job that afternoon was to look for picnickers or campers who might be violating the current ban on camp fires, and perhaps incidentally to see if he spotted anyone who might appear to be in trouble. From aloft there wasn't much he could do to enforce rules or to provide help, but he could report back and get some-one on the ground to take action. Sure enough, before long we spotted a pair of what appeared to be consenting adults next to a campfire. Charlie decided to convey a message from the air. He lowered a wing, put the plane into a steep "slip" (achieved with crossed controls), and slid down into the canyon that sheltered the offenders. He flew low over them, waggled his wings, and then climbed out of the canyon. We didn't have a chance to see if they got the message.

Charlie, had, of course, noticed before pulling off this stunt that he would have a way out. Among pilots, "box canyons" are famous killers. A pilot can find him-self between canyon walls too close together to allow the plane to turn around, and with an end wall too high to outclimb. Charlie loved to fly, and looked for any way to add a bit of spice to a flight. On this one, after completing his reconnaissance, instead of descending gradually from his altitude over the Jemez toward the Santa Fe airport, he flew level, arriving directly over the airport about 3,000 feet above the ground. Without giving me any advance warning, he pulled the nose up steeply, holding it there until the plane's speed fell below what was needed to sustain flight (a condition known as a stall—something determined by the aerodynamic condition of the plane, not the condition of the engine). Then, as the nose started to fall, Charlie moved the stick briskly as far to one side as he could, and at the same time pushed the opposite rudder as far forward as it would go. This is crossing the controls with a vengeance. The result, if it is executed properly, is a spin (sometimes known as a tailspin). With its nose pointing steeply downward, the plane corkscrews toward the ground like a winged maple seed. After spinning down 2,000 feet, Charlie stopped the spin, leveled out at traffic-pattern altitude, and turned around to flash me a big smile.

Spinning inadvertently, especially near the ground, and especially with an unseasoned pilot at the controls, is serious business. In the early days of flying, it accounted for many crashes and fatalities. Even now, spins ending tragically happen too often. It was precisely to prevent spins that Fred Weick left rudder pedals out of his Ercoupe. He didn't do it just to make his plane easier to fly, but to make it safer. A meritorious goal, but in the end, the need to be able to cross the controls for useful purposes trumped this safety consideration. An airplane (or glider) without rudder pedals is now an anachronism.

I have known other pilots like Charlie. They give the impression of being daredevils, but they aren't. They are skilled and they are careful. They always have in mind a way out if things don't quite go as planned. They might want to be viewed as cowboys, but they are calculating cowboys. They are fearless but not foolish. They know what they are doing and they don't risk their lives for no good reason. Mostly they die of old age, or at least some cause other than an airplane accident.

$\mathcal{P}rofile$

Charlie Boyd
1895-1974

Photo courtesy of the National Air and Space Museum, Smithsonian Institution (SI 2006-6849)

$\mathcal{W}$hen Charlie Boyd was born, in 1895, aviation consisted of occasional ascents in hot-air balloons and short hops in primitive gliders. When he died, in 1974, jet planes were spanning oceans. The big event between those two dates that nearly everyone knows about is Charles Lindbergh's non-stop flight from New York to Paris in 1927. But Lindbergh wasn't the first to fly the Atlantic. The first trans-Atlantic flight took place eight years earlier, and Charlie Boyd, although not part of the flying crew, had a hand in the success of that mission. On May 8, 1919, three giant flying boats, named NC-1, NC-3, and NC-4* (NC for Navy Curtiss), each with a crew of six, took off from

---

* NC-2 was left behind as an unflyable "hangar queen." She had graciously donated a wing to NC-1, whose own wing had been lost to surf when a storm had come up while she was at anchor in the bay.

the waters near Rockaway Beach, New York, close to the present site of JFK Airport. More than three weeks later, one of them, NC-4, touched down in the harbor of Plymouth, England, having hopscotched via Chatham, Massachusetts; Halifax, Nova Scotia; Trepassey, Newfoundland; Horta and Ponta Delgada in the Azores; and Lisbon, Mondego River, and Ferrol in Portugal. (NC-1 and NC-3 made forced landings on the ocean after covering most of the distance from Newfoundland to the Azores. NC-1 sank, but not before its crew members were rescued by a Greek freighter—embarrassing in a way because Navy destroyers were cruising in the vicinity to provide rescue services if needed. NC-3 miraculously stayed afloat despite damage and rough seas, and, more miraculously still, drifted two hundred miles to a harbor in the Azores, where the crew fired up its engines and taxied the last few miles. No air-crew lives were lost.)

In mid-March 1919, Charlie Boyd, a 23-year-old Navy Machinist's Mate, was sent to Rockaway to help get the four (later three) planes ready for the great adventure. These were *big* planes. Each had four 400-horsepower engines, carried 1,800 gallons of gas, weighed 14 tons loaded, and stretched 126 feet from wingtip to wingtip. A few months earlier, one of them, NC-1, had carried fifty-one men aloft (a planned fifty plus one stowaway), a record at the time. On May 1, a week before the NC's—affectionately called Nancys—took off, Charlie and other members of the ground support crew left New York on the converted mine sweeper *Aroostook* for Trepassey, Newfoundland, arriving there on May 3 as part of what the historian Richard K. Smith called the "great Naval invasion" of Trepassey.* On board the *Aroostook* were extra airplane engines and no end of assorted tools and equipment for the use of the support crew, as well as extra bunks and food for the larger-than-normal ship's complement. Charlie and his crew mates were expected to work their magic on the big planes and their engines before their long hop to the Azores, and then later to tend to their needs in England.

On May 10, two days after leaving New York, NC-1 and NC-3 reached Trepassey, where, as Smith put it, "gangs of machinist's mates" swarmed over them. NC-4 limped in five days later, on May 15, with one very sick engine and assorted other problems. Again the support crew "swarmed." They worked all night and all the next day, installing a new engine and fixing other problems. By late afternoon on the 16th, the three planes were ready. They roared down the bay and were on their way to the Azores.

Some time that night—the night of May 16-17—the *Aroostook's* captain weighed anchor and headed for Plymouth, England, intending to arrive there as soon as possible after the Nancys touched town. As it happened, he and the support crew, reaching Plymouth on May 23, had a week to relax before NC-4 made its triumphant if belated appearance. Talking to a reporter fifty years later,

---

* Richard K. Smith, *First Across!* (Annapolis, Maryland: Naval Institute Press, 1973). The *Aroostook* was the maintenance support ship. Some of the other ships in the "invasion" were destroyers that were to take up positions at fifty-mile intervals along the entire trans-Atlantic route. of the planes.

Charlie Boyd said that he and fourteen crew mates had been in Plymouth to welcome NC-4. When I first read that statement, before unearthing the chronology outlined here, I was mightily puzzled. How, I asked myself, could Charlie have serviced a plane just before its takeoff from North America and been in England to greet its arrival there? As Richard Smith put it, "An airplane was obviously not the quickest means of crossing the Atlantic in 1919."

The task of Charlie and his crew mates in Plymouth was to make sure NC-4 was in shape for some ceremonial flights around western Europe, then to take it apart and see to its shipment back to America, and finally to reassemble it in Central Park in New York City for an admiring public. The historical record does not make crystal clear that Charlie was part of the Central Park exhibition, but it seems likely, for he wrote in one Navy document* that he was stationed in New York City for the month of July 1919, his last month of service in the Navy. According to a newspaper article at the time, the support crew of NC-4 served as security guards around the plane twenty-four hours per day while it was on display in Central Park.

After his honorable discharge from the Navy on August 7, 1919, Charlie set about trying to fashion a career in the still very new field of aviation. For

---

* In this same document, the dates Charlie lists for his time in Rockaway, Trepassey, and Plymouth don't track exactly with the *Aroostook's* log, but he does record that his embarkation for overseas service was on the *Aroostook*. Some of what I report here as fact about Charlie's service are only my best surmises based on available evidence.

a while, it was touch and go. He had to work on automobiles as well as airplanes, but eventually he gave up auto repair and became a full-time pilot and aircraft mechanic.

Over the years, Charlie was strangely reluctant to talk about his role in the 1919 trans-Atlantic flight. Periodically, reporters tracked him down: in 1929 on the tenth anniversary of the event, in 1939 on the twentieth anniversary, in 1944 on the twenty-fifth anniversary, and again in 1969 on the fiftieth anniversary. The 1929 report says that Charlie agreed to be interviewed only after a friend urged him to. The 1939 report says he had to be reminded about the event before discussing it. He was a bit more voluble in 1969, but several still-living friends of Charlie say that he never talked with them about his role in the 1919 flight.

Nevertheless, it was evidently meaningful to Charlie, for he carefully preserved two souvenirs that are now in the possession of his step-grandson. One is a 1919 medal commemorating the "First Annual Aeronautical Expedition New York," attached to a red, white, and blue ribbon and mounted in a case that also contains a handwritten inscription by A. C. Read, the NC-4 pilot: "Presented to Chas J. Boyd by A. C. Read [who] Piloted the NC4, First Aircraft to Fly the Atlantic Ocean 1919." Charlie's other souvenir of that flight is a large barometer inside whose case is written, "Trans Atlantic NC 4 Flight May 16-31 . . .[with a list of en route stops] . . . C. J. Boyd M. M."

*C*harlie Boyd was born in Clinton, Missouri. The details of his early life are lost in the mists of time. There's no evidence that he attended college, although his later patents and his meticulous drawings in support of them suggest that he may have had some engineering training. In 1930 he secured a patent on an airplane with folding wings. Whether it was ever constructed I have not been able to ascertain. In 1936 he invented an automobile lubricator and, with the help of "several" traveling salesmen, sold more than three hundred of them around the Southwest: $7.50 for the large model, $3.75 for the small one. He reportedly made many other inventions.

Charlie joined the Navy in February 1918, some ten months after the U. S. entered World War I. His assignment as a machinist's mate presumably reflected mechanical skills that he already possessed, although, in the ways of the military, it could have been unrelated to particular skills. After he left the Navy in August 1919, he went back to the Midwest in search of opportunities in aviation, and the following April went to work as an airplane mechanic for Harry Rinker in Salina, Kansas. Rinker, who described himself on his letterhead as "Aviator," paid Charlie $45 per week to keep his one airplane flying. Through passenger rides, demonstrations, banner towing, photography, instruction, and lectures, Rinker hoped to make a living in his chosen profession of Aviator. When business slowed after a few months, he let Charlie go, and not too many months after that, folded up his operation.

I have not been able to find out when and how Charlie learned to fly. When he moved to Amarillo, Texas in 1927 it was to open a garage and filling station. By 1929 he was building an airplane in the back of his garage and by the late 1930s he was managing the Amarillo Municipal Airport. In 1938 he participated in a grand celebration called "National Air Mail Week." On May 19 of that year, an overwhelming 1,700 volunteer pilots flew a total of 134,000 miles for the United States Post Office Department to make it possible for every American in every small town to post an airmail letter and have it winging its way toward a destination on that same day. Charlie's assignment, in the course of a few hours that afternoon, was to fly from Amarillo to Happy, Texas to Tulia, Texas, to Silverton, Texas (serving also Quitaque, Texas), to Lubbock, Texas, and back to Amarillo, delivering and collecting mail pouches at every stop. (In Amarillo, commercial airliners took over.) In Happy, Charlie reported, "Field small and close to town; large crowd." In Silverton, he reported, "Field looked like a lake so landed north of town." Leaders of the towns with no designated landing strips furnished Charlie with drawings and instructions such as, "There is a small farm just west of the open space. This open space begins just South of the Section House and nearly even with the stock pens. If the pilot will land along side of the little farm he will avoid the wires along the railroad track." Speaking a few weeks later, Postmaster General James Farley was able to say that "not a single letter was lost nor a single pilot killed."

As early as 1930 Charlie was supplementing his automobile business by working on damaged airplanes, but it was some years after that before he could make a living in aviation alone. He moved from Amarillo to Santa Fe probably around 1944 and managed Boyd Aero Services there for thirty years. (He was 79 when he died in 1974.) Like so many in aviation, he had to piece together an income from a variety of sources. He taught students (including me). He flew passengers with the means and the need to get somewhere quickly. He flew the noted nature photographer Laura Gilpin around her beloved Southwest. He flew for the Forest Service and for the New Mexico Fish and Game Department.

One of his jobs for the Fish and Game Department was "planting" fingerling trout ("trout fry") in the cold, high-altitude lakes of the Sangre de Cristo Mountains (some above 11,000 feet). He practiced by dropping water from a special hopper on his Super Cub onto a small target at the Santa Fe Airport, and became widely admired for his precision in dropping thousands of the trout fry exactly where they should go in the middle of small lakes. Most of this work was done soon after dawn before turbulence and up and down drafts interfered. Even so, it was tricky work. I can see Charlie flashing his trademark smile at a drop done just right.

Everyone who knew Charlie has some story to tell. The manager of the airport in Las Vegas, New Mexico (not to be confused with Las Vegas, Nevada) told me one such story. On a dark and stormy night, Charlie was preparing to take off from Las Vegas to make his way back to Santa Fe. His friends in Las Vegas counseled him against it, urging him to stay the night and fly home in the morning. Charlie's answer was, "If the trains can make it, I can make it." What he intended to do was follow the Santa Fe Railroad line as it snaked through canyons and up and over Glorieta Pass on its way to the smoother terrain near Santa Fe. Charlie knew that there were signal lights along the track at one-mile intervals. He knew the country intimately and figured he could see from one signal light to the next and let them guide him home. It worked. He took off and he made it.

Another story I heard from at least two sources is the cat story. It seems that a wealthy woman had hired Charlie to fly her and her cat to a cat show in either Las Vegas, Nevada or Long Beach, California (memories differ). The cat was quite agitated in its cage as the flight got under way, but calmed down after a while. Somewhere over Arizona, the woman asked Charlie if it would be OK to let the cat out of the cage. He said, "Sure, but be careful. My upholstery is brand new." The cat, once free, became agitated again and started to claw the new upholstery on Charlie's Cessna 190. Not being able to catch the cat, Charlie rolled down the window on his side (this plane had windows like those in cars that were cranked up and down). The cat, in its rampage, leaped out the window and was last seen with all four paws stretched out as if anticipating a soft landing 3,000 feet below. According to one second-hand teller of this tale, Charlie, biting down on his unlit cigar, said, "Well, whadda ya wanna do now, lady?" She reputably answered, "Keep going. I've got to get me a new cat."

Charlie's obituary says he "was noted for his ability in stunt flying and in demonstrations as how not to fly an airplane." What that tells me is that he simply *loved* to fly. He loved to make people think he was reckless. Once, for instance, when a strong wind was blowing he lined up his Super Cub at the hangar pointing into the wind toward the big tetrahedron that indicates wind direction, roared toward it, hopped over it, and landed beyond it, all within the space of a few hundred feet. Charlie died old and in bed. He is known to have had only one mishap, when he snagged a power line while landing at night in Santa Fe. He did some damage to the airplane but not to himself—if you don't count the psychological impact.

*C*harlie was also noted among his flying peers in New Mexico for his abilities as a mechanic. He had no peer in repairing fabric-covered airplanes and had the unusual ability to weld aluminum. He had an A&P (aircraft and power plant) license that authorized him to repair planes, but not an IA (inspection authorization) license that allowed him to sign off on their airworthiness. For years he had an arrangement with Gilly de Baca in Las Vegas, New Mexico, whereby Charlie would do the work and Gilly (who had an IA license) would sign off on it. Gilly had so much respect for Charlie's work that he just did a quick walk-around and then took care of the paperwork. When Gilly retired, Charlie was in a fix—or thought he was—because his cantankerous personality had led to friction with all the other people in the flying business in the Santa Fe area. Here's the story of how things worked out all right after all, as told by Fred Duran, a mechanic and an IA who worked for, and later became the president of, Post Aviation, a principal fixed-base operator in Santa Fe.

"Charlie called the FAA and said, 'How am I going to get this plane inspected? Cuss, cuss.' And the guy at the FAA said, 'Well, the closest person to you is Fred Duran.'

'Where the hell is he?' Charlie said.

'Well, he's over at Post Aviation.'

'Well, how the hell is that going to work? I don't like those SOB's at Post.'

'Well, you'll like him. He's nice enough.'

"Charlie called me and you could tell he was just mad as hell over even having to call me. He said, 'You're Fred Duran, right? Well, I've got a Pawnee here to inspect. I did a major repair on it and it needs relicensing."

'Fine, Charlie. What's convenient for you?' He was taken aback that I wanted to know what his schedule was. He said, 'Well, I'd like to have it done by tomorrow.'

'What time of the day?' I said.

'Well, can you be here at 9:00 in the morning?'

"'Yeah, I'll be there.'

'Another thing,' he says, 'I don't know how to do paperwork. Gilly always did that for me.'

'Don't worry about it,' I said. 'I'll do it for you.'

"So I went over and opened the hangar door and this beautiful Pawnee's sitting there but it was buttoned up, not open as you'd expect it would be for inspection. And he says, 'I suppose you're going to ask me to open it up.'

'Charlie,' I said, 'When a whippersnapper like me wants to insult you by wanting you to open your plane to look at it, if I were you I'd take offense at that. I just need to see the log books. And I'll do a walk-around and admire your work.'

"Suddenly I could do no wrong. He was showing off all his work and how he re-covered the tail. It was a beautiful job. It really was. We got through the walk-around and went into his office. I did the paperwork. Nothing to do by then but I'd better go have lunch with him. Then after having lunch I had to see his shotgun loading equipment. Pretty much took me most of the afternoon to get away from him."

$\mathcal{A}$ ll of Charlie's flying compatriots seem to agree. He was a superb pilot, a superb mechanic, and an ornery cuss. But I guess he had a way with the ladies. According to Mary Lou Montgomery, the daughter-in-law of Charlie's second wife: "Charlie Boyd was a wonderful, kind-hearted person. He had lots of young friends. He knew everyone in Santa Fe."

-2-
Becoming A Pilot

After about three weeks, Charlie Boyd either got tired of me or got too busy with other things. I was passed laterally to another instructor, who, in turn, handed me off to another (still under Charlie's oversight). On August 8, 1953, five weeks into my flying career, I had logged eleven hours of dual instruction and was feeling about ready to solo. But events intervened, and that great moment didn't occur until December, four months later. Another great moment was looming on the calendar, my upcoming wedding. I traveled back to Princeton, my bride-to-be traveled with me to Los Alamos, we were married, we honeymooned in Colorado and Utah (in the $200 Chevrolet), and we drove to Bloomington, Indiana, where I was to take up my new duties at the university there.

Once we got settled, I made my way to the local airport, Kisters Field. I explained my small dilemma to John Myers, the airport manager: My airplane was 1,500 miles away and I wasn't authorized to fly it to Indiana. He put me in touch with a congenial undergraduate who had just earned his flying license and was eager to log more hours. For the price of a bus ticket to Santa Fe and gas money for the flight back, he was more than happy to do it. Come Thanksgiving time, he carried out the mission. In early December, an instructor in Bloomington took me through my paces, and on December 10, having logged twelve hours of dual instruction with four instructors, I soloed. After a short dual flight that day, the instructor said, casually, "I think I'll have a cup of coffee. Why don't you take it up." He ambled over to the operations shack as if totally unconcerned, and take it up I did. I was pretty sure he was glued to the window watching my takeoff and landing, but he hinted at no anxiety. Afterwards, I got the traditional congratulations from the few people who were gathered, but escaped their scissors, probably because I was wearing a dress shirt. According to tradition, the newly soloed pilot has his or her tee shirt cut off (yes, even if it's a her). With a marker pen, the shirt is labeled with the pilot's name and the date, and hung on the office wall.

Dual instruction doesn't end with the solo flight. By the time I took the exam for a pilot's license in February, I had accumulated eighteen hours of dual instruction, on top of 25 hours of solo time. Fifty years later, my log book shows that out of my total flight time of 4,504 hours (I stopped flying in 2003), 159 hours were flown with an instructor. These flights with instructors were for many purposes—checking out in new airplanes, learning to fly gliders, learning to fly on instruments, taking instrument competency check rides, and taking annual check rides in tow planes and gliders.

Today the average student pilot, before taking the private pilot exam, amasses more time, both dual and solo, than I did. I did not have to take a written exam or submit to "ground school" instruction. I did not have to learn how to navigate by radio or how to keep the plane upright in a cloud. I couldn't have: My airplane had no radio navigation equipment and had no gyroscopic instruments, which are necessary to retain control with no outside visibility. In fact, because I took my flight test at a small, uncontrolled, unpaved field in Franklin, Indiana, I didn't even have to use my rudimentary communications radio.

I used the rest of that academic year to build time, flying to various destinations in Indiana and in neighboring states, sometimes with a passenger, sometimes in a gaggle of two planes when a fellow pilot would rather fly his own plane than ride with me. A couple of times, I flew into Meigs field on the Chicago lakefront, a field later made famous as the home base in the Microsoft Flight Simulator program. When a friend gave me that program and I tried it out, I kept crashing on the runway or in Lake Michigan. I gave it up, deciding that flying airplanes was a lot easier than flying a simulator on a home computer. Naturally, when I had a "business" reason to fly, such as attending a meeting or giving a talk, I tried to go in my own airplane. My Ercoupe carried me to Ohio State University and to the University of Michigan that spring.

And, as I am about to narrate, painful though it is to do so, I made one flight to Washington, D.C.

It is said that along about 100 hours of experience, pilots are prone to get overconfident and to do stupid things, sometimes not surviving their stupidity. My turn to exhibit astonishing stupidity came after eighty hours of flying. I had to attend a meeting in Washington at the end of April 1954 and decided to fly myself there—in an airplane with no navigational radio, no gyroscopic instruments, and a communications radio that was marginal at best. I found a graduate student who wanted to come along and we set out on April 28. After stops in Cincinnati and Galipolis, Ohio, we had to call it a day in Elkins, West Virginia because clouds sat low over the mountains farther east. We found a motel within walking distance of the field. In the morning we checked the weather. The clouds of the night before were gone and the forecast was for scattered to broken clouds east of the mountains over Virginia, with ceilings (distances from the ground to the bases of the clouds) of 1,000 to 2,000 feet. It sounded OK and we charged into the air. (It shouldn't have sounded OK. "Scattered" is encouraging; "broken" is not.)

Then, as so often happens, reality didn't match the forecast. As we cleared the higher mountains, we saw that the clouds to the east were neither scattered nor broken. They were solid, in a flat stratus layer that seemed to stretch indefinitely ahead of us. The sensible thing, of course, would have been to execute a 180-degree turn and fly back to Elkins. Instead, I pushed on until I was sure (pretty sure), according to the clock, that I was past the high ground and over the low country of central Virginia. I descended to just above the top of the stratus layer in order to get some sense of how thick it might be. My altimeter showed about 2,500 feet above sea level. Since I expected the ground in this area to be around 300 to 500 feet above sea level, and since the ceiling was forecast to be at least 1,000 feet, I reasoned (if you can call it reasoning) that the cloud layer could hardly be more than 1,000 feet thick. I thought (if you can call it thinking) that I should be able to descend safely through it without proper instrumentation. I leveled off just skimming the top of the cloud layer, then throttled back to a low power setting and held the speed to about 85-90 miles per hour, enough to assure a fairly brisk descent. Down we went. Indeed the cloud was only about 1,000 feet thick, but it seemed an awfully long time to get through it as we slid down through the murk. When green fields appeared mistily beneath us, we were not flying level anymore, but spiraling downward in a bank of about 30 degrees.

I quickly leveled out, giving no hint to my passenger that there was the least danger or that this sort of thing wasn't something pilots do every day. "Well," I said to him, "with this much haze and this low a ceiling, we should not try to fly on to Washington. Let's look for an airfield." Of course, I had only the sketchiest idea of where we were. I headed northeasterly and—good luck— almost at once an airport appeared, a small one with grass runways. We landed, tied down, and then learned that we were in Culpeper, Virginia.

By now, you can surmise that this tale of ineptitude and bad judgment has a happy ending. In fact, it has an amusing little twist.

A bus brought me and my passenger to Washington that afternoon. My passenger went his way (he had not planned to return with me in any case) and I checked into the hotel where I had a reservation. I learned that the first bus to Culpeper in the morning left at 5:00 a.m. I caught it. The bus driver was kind enough to drop me a relatively short walk from the airport, which was unmanned and unguarded at that hour. I made my way to my plane, untied it, did the pre-flight, and took off for Washington, intending to call Washington National Airport when I was about thirty miles from it and get clearance to land there. But my troubles were not at an end. My radio failed to work. No response. My map showed a little suburban airport in northern Virginia not far from Washington National. I landed there and found it, too, unmanned. Moreover it seemed to have no public telephone. I walked out to a neighboring road, stuck out my thumb, and caught a ride a mile or so to where a public phone was visible on a corner. From that phone I called the control tower at Washington National and explained my situation, asking if I could land in order to get my radio fixed. The controller could not have been more accommodating. "Can you be over the field at 11:00?" he asked. I checked my watch, and said, "Yes, I think so."

"Good," he said. "Fly across the field heading west to east at 1,200 feet, at exactly 11:00 o'clock, and look for a light. Make a right-hand pattern to land on runway 3."

I rushed back to the road, stuck out my thumb again, and was lucky again. I got back to my plane and into the air with a bit of time to spare, circled near the small airport, then headed east as directed. Looking down toward the tower, I saw, sure enough, a green light aimed at me, signaling that I was cleared to land. Once I was on the ground, a "Follow Me" jeep led me to a parking space. The radio got fixed and I departed two days later. To this day, I have never met another pilot who landed at National Airport without a functioning radio.

I guess you could call the return trip anticlimactic. It took seven-and-a-half hours in the air bucking a head wind, with fuel stops in Huntington, West Virginia, and Lexington, Kentucky, before settling onto the grass in Bloomington.

Descending through that cloud near Culpeper was not the only dumb thing I have ever done in the air, but it is probably the dumbest. I never tempted fate quite so blatantly again. One among my serious errors that day was trusting that the ceiling over Virginia would be about as forecast. It didn't take me long to learn that weather forecasting, at least for a particular location, is full of uncertainty. Remarkably, although area forecasting improved greatly over the next fifty years, predicting conditions at a particular airport for a particular time is about as chancy now as it was then. The atmosphere is a complex and tricky system that can outfox the best computers. The butterfly effect is real.*

In the years ahead, I did become a pretty good and pretty careful pilot. Apart from the general

---

* It was the MIT meteorologist Edward Lorenz who famously asked, in 1972, "Does the Flap of a Butterfly's Wings in Brazil set off a Tornado in Texas?"

accumulation of experience, the biggest contributor to safety (and sensible behavior) was earning
an instrument rating, something I did in 1960,
adding a commercial license a year later. The
instrument rating, if kept alive through regular use
and/or regular check rides with instructors, allows
a pilot to fly through clouds under control from the
ground, and to make instrument approaches to
many airports. Needless to say, using the rating
requires that the planes one flies have all the right
instruments to make such flight practical and safe.

In 1958, before I had an instrument rating, I had an
experience that illustrates well the difference in safety
between flying (legally) through clouds and ducking
under them. I was on my way from Bedford,
Massachusetts, near Boston, to College Park, Maryland,
a suburb of Washington, DC, flying an Ercoupe, which,
like my earlier one, had no gyroscopic instruments.
Because ceilings were low in the northeast (not quite so
low around Washington), I planned to make an end run
around New York City, heading west across Connecticut,
crossing the Hudson River well north of New York, then
angling southward toward my destination. As
I approached the Hudson, I was "scud-running" under
a 1,000-foot ceiling with visibility of two or three miles.
The Hudson, where I chose to cross it, was wide—too
wide to see from one side to the other on that particular
morning. Out over the river, the water, the horizon, and
the sky merged into a single murky grayness. Descending
quickly to 500 feet, I could make out the water surface
well enough to tell which direction was up. I pushed

ahead until trees and houses appeared on the far shore. I landed at the first airport I could find, in New City, New York, and waited for the weather to improve (which it did). Had I had an instrument rating (and a suitable airplane), the flight would have been safe and simple. Instead, it was pushing to the very limit or a little beyond the limit of safe flying.

There. Almost full disclosure. Now I have described two occasions when my poor judgment put me in grave danger. Descending through the cloud layer near Culpeper and feeling my way across the scarcely visible Hudson happened early in my career, a high-risk time for any pilot. A third near-brush with disaster came later, more the result of negligence than poor judgment—if there's a difference—and fortunately ended without mishap, too. I'll come to it in Chapter 7. Every close call remains vivid.

By the time I reached 1,000 hours a dozen years after my first flight (ten years of flying, actually, because of two leaves of absence for study and research in Europe), I felt that I had become a reasonably safe and a reasonably sensible pilot. When I stopped flying after fifty years, I estimate that I had made 8,000 landings, give or take a thousand, at more than 450 different airports and landing strips, from Burris Ranch in New Mexico (where the strip doubles as a driveway) to O'Hare International in Chicago, flying some 55 different models of airplanes and gliders, the biggest of the lot capable of holding six people, the smallest accommodating the pilot alone with no passengers. The airports and air strips where I touched down were in 42 states plus Mexico and Canada. Only once did I damage an airplane (actually a glider) on landing.

Another time, I came perilously close to landing a retractable-gear airplane with the gear up—the kind of event that has embarrassed many a pilot. On that occasion, I was just about to land at Washington National Airport (this time with a radio) when, at the last moment, the tower asked me to change to a different runway—probably because a following jet was getting too close. That entailed turning and climbing a few hundred feet before turning again and descending again. I raised the landing gear for the maneuver and was close to touchdown on the revised runway when at last I remembered that the gear was now up. I was saved by a little mental check list that I liked to run through on final approach. It's called GUMP, and stands for Gas (is the correct tank feeding the engine?), Undercarriage (is it down?), Mixture (is it set correctly for the airport's altitude?), and Prop (is the pitch set properly in case power needs to be applied to go around?).

Then there is the hazard of an engine quitting in the air. This happened to me only twice—the same engine, actually, quitting twice for the same reason, the accumulation of ice blocking air from entering the carburetor. Since the plane in question (an Aeronca Champ) had no electric starter and had to be hand-cranked, having it stop in flight created a challenge. The first time it happened, I was high over the Indiana countryside practicing spins. (Why spin on purpose? To reduce the surprise and alarm factor in case of some future inadvertent spin. And because it's fun.) So, for the first time in the air, I was looking at a stationary propeller. Fortunately, I had room enough to dive, causing the propeller to spin and enabling me to restart the engine. The second time it happened, with the same plane, I was in the traffic pattern at a small airport in Hinsdale, Illinois, on a frigid January day in 1957. I was able to glide down and land on the runway in what is known as a dead-stick landing. (It's actually the engine, not the stick, that is dead.) Then I had to get out, spin the prop by hand, jump back in the plane before it left me behind, and taxi to parking. Glider pilots like to say that gliders are safer than power planes because they don't have an engine to quit.

$\mathcal{P}rofile$

John Myers
(1916-1991)

Photo courtesy of Chuck & Dow Myers

" When John wasn't at the airport, what did he do?" I asked John Myers' sons Chuck and Dow.

"He went to the airport," answered Chuck.

"And took us with him," added Dow. "He needed the extra hands."

"I can hardly remember a single vacation as a child," said Chuck. "That airport was Dad's life. We grew up there."

Since Chuck is now a professional pilot and Dow, an enforcement officer with Indiana's Department of Natural Resources, expresses regret that he didn't complete his flight training, their father's single-minded dedication to aviation must have drawn them toward flying more than it pushed them away from it.

I knew from personal experience that John Myers was wedded to his job as manager of the Bloomington, Indiana airport. Wedded, as "in sickness and in health"—in his case, in good weather and bad, in lean budget years (mostly) and generous budget years (occasionally), in constructive and corrosive political climates, in accident-free years and years with tragic deaths. Of course, being wedded and being in love are not always the same thing. But John was in love with his job. When he retired in 1982 at the age of 65, he had just about as much bounce and enthusiasm as he had when he started the job twenty-seven years earlier, in 1955. His carrot-topped head had lost none of its curly luster, and he was still trim. His smile came as easily, and the light in his eye was as strong.

It was only in the first few years of John's job as an airport manager that I lived in Bloomington and flew from Kisters Field (now more blandly named Monroe County Airport). But often in the years that followed, I stopped in Bloomington for gas or a vending-machine meal, and made a point of greeting John when I could. If it was winter, he might be exceeding the speed limit on his snow plow as he careened around the airport. If it was summer, he might be riding his mower in shirt sleeves, keeping the one remaining grass strip in perfect condition. If I didn't find him, it might be because he was out ferrying Herman Wells, the president of Indiana University, somewhere or was up with a student or was in the private hangar of one of the local corporations, tinkering with an airplane. The one place I rarely found him was behind a desk. Yet somehow he accomplished the needed paper work, and somehow cajoled the airport board and the county into putting up money for a longer paved runway, a control tower, an ILS* approach, and new hangars. (The Federal government did its part, too.)

John Myers was born in Bloomington in 1916, and died there in 1991, at 75. When he left high school in 1934 at 17, he went to work in a local quarry (the area is famous for its limestone—if you don't believe it, have a look at the Indiana University campus). As he told it years later to a friend, he woke up so sore and stiff after his first day on the job that he decided that there must be an easier way to earn a living. Instead of going back to the quarry for a second day, he joined the Navy, and spent the next twenty years in Naval aviation.

John's Navy record says he completed three years of high school. His sons say he graduated. Since, as I knew first hand, he was both smart and conscientious, I can't imagine that he was having any trouble with his studies. Perhaps there was something in this teenager's life—other than the quarry—from which he wanted to escape. We'll never know.

John's Navy record doesn't reveal how he got into aviation. Then, as now, pilots were almost all college

---

* Instrument landing system, making it possible to land when the ceiling was as low as 200 feet and the visibility as low as half a mile. Before the ILS was installed, there was a more rudimentary radio landing system with requirements for ceiling and visibility both about twice as great.

graduates, so he had no chance to enter pilot training. Maybe someone recognized his mechanical aptitude. Maybe he himself applied to become an airplane mechanic. Maybe he was assigned at random. In any case, the Navy trained him to become an aircraft mechanic, and he must have been good at it. In later life, the only thing John liked more than fixing airplanes was flying them.

John's initial training—in boot camp—was in Norfolk, Virginia. Like every other fresh enlistee, he started on the lowest rung of the ladder, as an Apprentice Seaman. He emerged from boot camp as a Seaman second class, and was sent to the USS Lexington for a week (who knows why), then to the USS Saratoga for six months and on to the USS Black Hawk for another half year. (The Lexington and Saratoga were aircraft carriers, the Black Hawk, a destroyer tender.) This was, in principle, a period of peace, but it wasn't quite, since at the time the Japanese were busy invading China and the Chinese were busy fighting back. That was, in fact, a very bloody war, and the United States wasn't wholly above the fray. In 1936 and 1937, John served on a destroyer, the John D. Ford, and earned a China Medal for the time that ship spent in the waters off China. Whether he was shot at or did any shooting the record doesn't show.

John's sons inherited a China scrap book from their father that looks all the world like the photographic record of any curious American tourist. It contains pictures of Chinese cities, Chinese peasants, and Chinese buildings, as well as the Great Wall of China.

There's no record of how John took these pictures or when (except we know it was in the 1930s). The scrapbook only reveals that John had a great curiosity about China and took advantage of the opportunity the Navy gave him to check it out.

Early in 1938, John was assigned to a heavy cruiser, the USS Indianapolis, and promoted to Aviation Machinist's Mate third class. Yes, a cruiser, not an aircraft carrier. At that time, the Indianapolis and cruisers like it kept a complement of four scouting aircraft on board. These were seaplanes that were lowered to the water by a crane for takeoff and hoisted back on board after landing. There's no evidence that John flew any of these, but he must have been itching to do so.

With a war in Europe under way and rumblings in the Pacific, John ascended through the enlisted grades more swiftly—to Aviation Machinist's Mate second class in 1940, to Aviation Machinist's Mate first class in 1941, and to Chief Petty Officer (Aviation Chief Machinist's Mate, to give the exact title) in 1942. At that level, as a sailor without a college degree, he encountered the Navy's version of a glass ceiling. It was many years later, around 1950, that he was finally named a Warrant Officer, a rank to which enlisted sailors with at least thirteen years of service and specialized technical knowledge can ascend (but ascend no further). In his case, it seems likely that the rank was awarded to recognize the fact that he was a pilot and an expert on aircraft maintenance.

During the first part of the U.S. involvement in World War II, John found himself in a patrol squadron that flew slow, heavy, reliable PBY seaplanes on patrol duty on both the Atlantic and Pacific sides of the Panama Canal Zone, mainly looking for submarines. One can surmise that on some of these flights, which could last up to thirteen hours, John volunteered to go along in order to provide relief to a pilot by handling the controls for him for some part of the flight. It's only speculation, but it seems likely that as time went on, he learned to take off and land the airplanes as well as to handle them in the air (all this, of course, in addition to his skill in maintaining the planes).

In mid-1942, John was assigned to an aviation training unit in Norfolk (and given the "Chief" title), no doubt to put all his knowledge to work as a teacher. After two-and-a-half years there, he moved on for briefer assignments in St. Louis and San Diego. When the war ended, in the summer of 1945, he was back with an operational unit, "AirPac Pool" (Air Forces, Pacific Fleet).

While still in the Navy, John capitalized on the abilities as a pilot that he had somehow acquired (his Navy records are totally silent on how and when he did it). In 1947, he soloed a Piper Cub in Norfolk and a month later gained his Private Pilot license. The next year he earned a Commercial license and a flight instructor's rating. And the year after that (1949) he added the multi-engine rating. Somewhere along the way, he also earned an A&P (Aircraft and Powerplant) license and an IA (Inspector's Authorization), enabling him to certify the airworthiness of airplanes. (Military skills don't transfer automatically to these civilian designations. He had to demonstrate his skills all over again.)

John was moving fast on the personal front, too. In late 1947, June Freund (pronounced FREE-und), a pretty eighteen-year-old from San Diego, was visiting her sister Kay and her sister's husband Rudy in Norfolk, where Rudy was a Navy buddy of John. Rudy thought it would be a good idea to introduce John (31, and eligible) to June, and June to John. June can't recall now whether John proposed on their first date, but she's sure it was within the first week after they met. She seemed as willing as he to jump. Presto. They were engaged. In early 1948, no more than a couple of months after first meeting, they hopped in a car and started west. They got no farther than South Carolina—a day's drive—in the unmarried state. After finding an official there to perform the ceremony, they proceeded on to San Diego and John's new assignment in wedded bliss. Their first child, a daughter Ellen, arrived on Christmas day that year.

When I spoke to June in 2005, I asked her what it had been like to be married to someone in love with aviation. "Oh, it was wonderful," she said. "Just great. You know, he taught me to fly—just in case. And did you know that he built an airplane himself? It took a year." I hadn't known.

When John left the Navy in 1954, he and June and the four children they had accumulated in six years of marriage headed back to John's native Indiana town, Bloomington, where they bought a 167-acre farm.

John promptly rented the acreage to local farmers—keeping only a garden and a few cows and chickens for his own family—and headed for the nearest airport.

Here's how a local pilot, Len Keen, described meeting John: " I had just arrived in Bloomington in the fall of 1954, to start work as a pilot for Rogers Construction. I went to the airport, and the first person I met was John Myers. He was sitting on a bench, just sitting there looking out over the airport. We got to talking and I invited him along on my first flight in Rogers' Twin Bonanza. It didn't take me long to learn that John was an excellent pilot and an excellent mechanic."

John secured work as an airplane mechanic and flight instructor, and within a year was hired by the county to manage the airport, a job he held for twenty-seven years. It was in the early part of that service that he checked me out in an Aeronca Champ—the same one whose engine decided to stop running while I was doing spins over Bloomington and while approaching the Hinsdale, Illinois airport.

In Bloomington, John and June had two more children. The first of these (their fifth) was a girl who died in infancy. The next (their sixth and last) was a son, Paul, who, like his older brothers Dow, Chuck and Bert, was drafted for airport work as soon as he was old enough. According to Chuck, "We learned how to drive by the time we were big enough to see over the steering wheel because on weekends and holidays we had to plow snow or drive tractors and mow the grass. It seemed like it just snowed on weekends and holidays, when we were available."

When John retired in 1982, it was under a cloud. His two youngest sons had been helping themselves to gas and some other supplies at the airport, and it came to light—not a huge amount, about $4,000 worth over five years, but big enough to be a painful embarrassment, or worse. To shield his boys, John said he had authorized what they did. He was allowed to resign without penalty.

That didn't stop him from flying and working on planes. Aviation remained his life. When he died almost ten years later, he had logged some 12,000 hours flying airplanes and who knows how many hours working on them. He flew up until two weeks before his death. "He wasn't sick," his older sons told me, "he just wore out."

Here's a tribute I heard from his old friend Len Keen. It wasn't delivered at the funeral. It wasn't part of a eulogy. It was just a remark Len made to me in conversation. "When I was coming back to Indiana in nasty winter weather, I always knew I could get into Kisters Field. Weir Cook was much less reliable. [Weir Cook is the main airport serving Indianapolis.] John would stay up all night plowing the runways if he had to."

-3-

Soaring

I didn't intend to become a glider pilot. It just
happened.

One of the reasons I liked being President of New
Mexico Tech in Socorro was that it gave me lots of
reasons to fly. Not long after I arrived there in the
summer of 1975, I went out to the local airport, and
told the airport manager, Ray Smith,* that I would
need to fly hither and yon but had no plane of my
own. "Don't worry, Ken," he said, "I'll keep you
flying." And he did. Among other jobs, Ray bought
and sold planes, and he let me rent anything from his
current inventory, always at a fair price. (In fact, he
let me do the bookkeeping. At the end of each month,
I figured out how much I owed him and sent him
a check.) In the course of my first year in Socorro,
I flew Cessna models 172, 177, 182, and 206, a Piper

---

* Ray Smith's profile begins on page 149

Comanche, a Piper Lance, a Piper Arrow, a Piper Super Cub, and a Beechcraft Bonanza.

Then, in the spring of that first academic year, an intriguing new plane arrived in town. It was home-made. The Navy, which provided funds for thunderstorm research at New Mexico Tech, had agreed to convert one of its drones (a zero-passenger plane) to a single-seat experimental aircraft whose purpose would be to fly into thunderstorms lugging a bunch of instruments to find out exactly what was going on inside the storms. Every pilot knew, some from hard personal experience, what thunderstorms held—lightning, rain, hail, monster up and down drafts, and bone-jarring turbulence. But there had been surprisingly little in the way of careful measurements of these things. Thus the plan was hatched to make the Special Purpose Technical Vehicle for Atmospheric Research, or SPTVAR (lovingly pronounced Spitfire) and have the Tech group use it to learn more.

The drone had been constructed using the body and wings of a Schweizer 2-32 glider—the largest in the Schweizer family—with a 200-horsepower engine and a tricycle landing gear bolted on. A company headed by J. William Bullock* in Colorado Springs was commissioned to turn the drone into a piloted aircraft and add the wires and hardware necessary to make it serve its intended purpose. Bill had flown atmospheric research missions before, including deliberate penetration of thunderstorms, and was well known to some of the New

---

* Bill Bullock's profile begins on page 173

Mexico Tech researchers. He was small in stature (5' 7", 145 lb) and had a fair-sized ego. He made the cockpit large enough—just large enough—to accommodate someone of about his size. He was to fly the plane and had no great interest in expanding its roster of pilots.

Like Charlie Boyd and other professional pilots I have met, Bill Bullock projected a devil-may-care fearlessness. (He once said to me, in his best John Wayne voice, "When those golf-ball-sized hailstones started hammering my windshield, it got my attention.") And, like Charlie Boyd and the others who outlived the actual cowboys of the air, he was a careful, skilled pilot who flew always with a safety margin, always with a way out. It's more than just an instinct for self-preservation that keeps pilots like Bill Bullock alive to enjoy old age. It's true professionalism, skill combined with respect for the elements and the drive to learn more and more and fly better and better.

We physicists love the Navy. Right after World War II, it became a leader in government largesse to physics, and kept up its good work in the years that followed. When Bill Bullock and "Spitfire" arrived in Socorro, the plane remained the property of the Navy, and a research administrator in Washington kept a fatherly eye on it. Among the researchers in Tech's premier atmospheric research group was Charlie Moore, who was burning to learn more about the insides of thunderstorms and was glad to have Bill

Bullock, apparently of sound mind, eager to fly into the worst that the New Mexico sky had to offer.

Once the plane was in Socorro, Bill and Charlie and others from the thunderstorm group went about hanging an assortment of instruments from its wings—to measure electric fields, temperature, raindrop and hailstone size, amount of precipitation, and so on. Observing all of this, it occurred to me that there must be times when the plane needed to be test-flown in good weather or needed to be ferried to another airport for service. I told Charlie Moore that I would be willing to handle such chores to relieve Bill Bullock of total responsibility. Charlie knew that Bill would not consider this such a wonderful plan, but Charlie himself liked the idea and—using the same persuasive powers that worked with the Navy—convinced Bill to consider it. To assure himself that I, a well-meaning amateur, might fly his plane without damaging it, Bill flew right-seat with me in one of the higher-performance Cessnas on the field. "For an amateur," he pronounced after that flight, "you are a pretty good pilot. It's OK."

Then there was the Navy. Charlie Moore sought the permission of his research mentors in Washington for me to fly the plane. These gentlemen put their heads together and came up with an answer: Yes—provided Dr. Ford has a license to fly gliders. (The airplane's wings, you see, were glider wings.) Well, I had no such license, but the Navy provided an interesting solution to that problem. It would cover the cost of my glider training. On April 28, 1976, I had my first glider lesson. On June 9 I soloed. On July 25 I became a licensed glider pilot. On

August 7, having met the Navy's condition, I flew the "Spitfire."

My glider training took place at Coronado Airport, a field on the northern fringe of Albuquerque that catered to private pilots and their planes. Coronado's one paved runway parallels the nearby Albuquerque-Santa Fe highway. Not far distant to the east are the towering Sandia Mountains, rising precipitously more than 5,000 feet above the valley floor. The area offers superb conditions for soaring in the spring and summer. Several of my training flights lasted more than an hour, and they could have lasted longer. On a typical day, uneven heating of the ground by the sun generates "thermals"—rising columns of air—here and there across the valley floor by noon. More thermals pop up over the sides of the mountains. A glider pilot need only find one of these to stay up, or, with luck, glide from one thermal to another without losing too much altitude in the sinking air between them. Besides thermals, another source of lift was the upsweep of a west wind encountering the Sandias.

On one training flight, I was flying along the mountain crest, at an altitude close to 11,000 feet, within hailing distance of tourists on the crest a short distance below, and thinking how marvelous it was to be so far above the sea, yet so close to people and trees. My instructor tapped me on the shoulder. "No farther east," he said, with a tone of urgency. I was too pleased with myself and this wonderful flight to be thinking carefully. Lift, when you've got it, can be intoxicating. I knew at once what he meant. Had we strayed over to the downwind side of the crest, we might well have encountered sinking air, in which case there would be no getting back up and over the crest and returning to Coronado. Instead we would have glided down the east slope and landed who knows where, many miles from where we wanted to be. I banked back toward the west and we made our way to Coronado.

Because I already had a license to fly powered planes, the requirements for getting a glider license were not onerous. I needed ten solo landings, the written recommendation of my instructor, and a flight test and oral test by a licensed examiner, who had to be someone other than the recommending instructor. Within six weeks, I had accomplished the ten landings and some five-and-a-half hours of solo time in the air, and secured the needed recommendation. I had also decided that soaring was so much fun that I would keep at it even after meeting the Navy's condition. So I joined the Albuquerque Soaring Club and arranged to be tested in one of the Club's gliders in Moriarty, New Mexico. Moriarty is a tiny town forty miles east of Albuquerque at an elevation of 6,200 feet. This high up, runways need to be long, and Moriarty's strip (then grass) stretched for nearly a mile.

The examiner I drew was the legendary glider pilot Al Santilli, who, at that time, had already logged thousands of hours in gliders (by the time he turned 90, in 2004, he had log books bulging with 6,000 hours, and he was still flying). Al, as I quickly learned, was a born teacher. The oral part of my exam consisted mostly of listening, not answering. (One of the things said by members of the Club—affectionately—was that if you were in a glider and needed to find lift when Al Santilli was on the ground, fly to a place directly above him.) Although not trained as a meteorologist, there wasn't much about weather he didn't know. I managed to pass the flight test, and Al became my mentor and friend as I tried to improve my skills for the next nine years until I moved away from New Mexico. After several of my unsuccessful efforts to fly a glider 500 kilometers, Al lectured me on what I might have done wrong and always concluded with "Keep trying." We kept in touch, and he urged me on until finally I did make it.

When first learning to fly a tail-dragger with rudder pedals, I had to overcome my kiddie-car syndrome, as I recounted in Chapter 1. With gliders, a different anxiety dogged me at first. In a power plane, if you flare for landing a bit late and bounce when you touch town, you can apply some power and make the second touchdown a smooth one. If you make the mistake of approaching a short strip too high and too fast, you can apply power, gain some altitude, go around, and do better the second time. And if you are about to land and find the strip blocked by a departing or taxiing plane (or a Jeep, or a deer), again you can apply power, abort the landing, and try it again. In short, the question that bothered me was: How can I count on making good landings and safe landings without an engine?

As I soon learned, there was no real basis for my anxiety. A glider is different, in ways that make it possible to get down smoothly without incident (and, of course, without an engine). Almost all gliders have "spoilers" that can be deployed above or below the wings to greatly increase drag and cause the glider to descend along a steep path. The pilot, sensing a path that is too high, can extend the spoilers and descend steeply in order to touch down near the beginning of the runway. In a typical approach, spoilers are adjusted during the descent to control the angle and the touchdown point. It is not difficult in general to hit a target point on the runway within a hundred feet. The bounce, too, is an uncommon event. Sitting in a glider, the pilot's rump is no more than a foot off the ground just before touchdown, so it's relatively easy to gauge the height and accomplish a smooth landing. As to avoiding a taxiing plane or errant Jeep that suddenly appears where you were planning to land, that is rarely a problem either. The glider can be set down on grass beside a runway instead of on the runway, and it needs relatively little real estate on which to touch down and roll to a stop. Five hundred feet is normally enough. So the glider pilot trying to avoid something on the ground can land short of the obstruction, land beside it, or land beyond it. In fact, on a busy summer afternoon at a gliderport, it's not unusual for a glider pilot approaching for a landing to see a couple of other gliders on the ground that have landed moments earlier. Since they can't taxi out of the way, they must sit there awaiting someone to come and tow them aside. Entanglements in situations like this are extremely rare.

SOARING

One of the gliding techniques I learned from Al Santilli is porpoising, which is the art of alternately raising the glider's nose (to go slower) and lowering it (to go faster) while flying straight ahead, the intent being to minimize the loss of altitude while covering a given distance. Porpoises apparently have great fun porpoising. The glider pilot hoping to get back to the home airport late in the afternoon despite being uncomfortably close to the ground and despite the absence of any strong thermal lift, is more likely to be sweating than having fun. But he or she will smile as broadly as a happy porpoise if the technique pays off and the landing takes place on the airport, not in the adjoining neighborhood.

One of Al's old friends, Paul MacCready (born 1925), introduced the "speed to fly" concept (to which I return in Chapter 5). For every glider, there is a best speed to fly through rising air, sinking air, and still air to minimize the loss of altitude over a given distance. Actually, MacCready had in mind a more sophisticated concept, the speed to fly through sinking air between thermals to minimize the total *time* for a cross-country task that includes many ups and downs. That's what's important in competition flying. More or less the same idea applies to flying straight ahead through areas where the air is rising slightly, sinking slightly, or doing neither, when the pilot's goal is just to reach the airport, not necessarily in the shortest time.

Imagine that you are five miles from your home airport. It's late in the day, there are no more strong thermals, and you are 1,200 feet above the airport's

53

elevation. Will you make it? If you can maintain a 30-to-1 descent profile, you will lose about 900 feet in five miles, arriving 300 feet above the airport. Definitely dicey. Various factors could make you and the ground meet before you get there. So you point toward the airport and adjust your speed moment to moment. When you encounter a bit of weak lift, you pull back on the stick and slow down. When you encounter a bit of weak sink, you push forward on the stick and speed up. If you are Al Santilli, you will sense exactly what speed to fly for each condition you meet during those five miles, and you are likely to arrive over the airport at a comfortable height of, say, 600 feet. That's porpoising.

_T_ wo days after Al Santilli decided that I deserved a glider license, I went up with Bill Bullock in a Piper Lance, a retractable-gear plane many notches above a Cub, for a biennial check ride. He put me through my paces and decided again that it was not too great a risk to the property of the United States Government to let me fly "Spitfire." At the next opportunity, ten days later, after an intervening trip to the east coast in that same Lance, I shoe-horned myself into Bill Bullock's pride and joy, listened to his last-minute admonitions, and took my first flight—two flights, actually, so I could practice a couple of landings. All went reasonably well. For a "home-built," it handled normally with no surprises. This was the first time—but not the last—that I flew in a single-seat pow-ered airplane. I always found it a little unsettling—and just a bit exciting—to take off in a plane that I had not first flown with an experienced pilot beside me or behind me.

A few days later, I took "Spitfire" up for two more short flights and two more landings. I was ready to do my duty to the Navy and the Tech researchers. But, for reasons that I can't now reconstruct, I never flew the plane again. Yet, it was because of "Spitfire" and the United States Navy that I became a glider pilot.

$\mathcal{M}$uch about flying gliders is the same as flying power planes. Much is different. In both, if you want to lower the nose, you push forward on a stick or wheel. In both, if you want to bank to the right, you move the stick or wheel to the right. In both, if you want to pull the nose to the left (or maintain coordinated flight as you enter a left turn), you push with the left foot against a rudder pedal. In short, they have the same control surfaces that aircraft have had for a hundred years: ailerons, elevator, and rudder. And both have the same kind of stability. If you push the nose of a power plane or glider downward and let go of the controls, the nose will come up again of its own accord. If you slew the nose left or right with the rudder and take your feet off the pedals, the nose will straighten itself out. Both also have the same *lack* of stability for banking. In either kind of aircraft, if you lower a wing and let go of the controls, the wing, in general, won't right itself. In fact, over time, it may even steepen its bank. This can give rise to the well-named graveyard spiral. If a pilot can't see a horizon outside the plane and has no gyroscopic instruments (or no ability to use them), the aircraft can enter a steepening spiral whose final outcome may be collision with the ground or water. This can happen in a cloud, or it can happen at night in perfectly clear weather over water or unpopulated land. It is believed to be what led to the untimely death of John F. Kennedy, Jr. in 1999. It's what happened to me—with time for recovery before it got out of hand—near Culpeper, Virginia.

Despite all the similarities, there are some significant differences between gliders and airplanes (apart from the obvious difference in motive power). Being generally slower, the glider tends to need more robust motions of the controls to make it do one's bidding. The glider is likely to be slicker, so that in still air it loses altitude at a very parsimonious rate. (The Space Shuttle is a glider that breaks this rule. Its rate of descent rivals that of a rock.) To me the greatest difference between gliders and airplanes is in the level of skill required to be really good at flying the things. After a few hundred hours, with an instrument rating, and with regular practice, a power pilot can get safely from one place to another and has about as much finesse as he or she is ever going to achieve. (Judgment is another matter. It matures over a longer time.) For a glider pilot, the room for improvement in skill is limitless. Glider pilots are like athletes. They can be like kids tossing a ball back and forth in the backyard, or like softball competitors at the company picnic (that's where I am), or like Big Leaguers in the World Series. Athletes at both ends of the spectrum can throw a ball and catch it. Glider pilots at both ends of the spectrum can stay up on a good day and put the glider down at an intended spot. Otherwise they don't have much in common.

What, exactly, is the skill that the best of the glider pilots possesses (a skill that I am a very long way from having)? It is finely tuned senses, judgment based on countless prior flights, and (as with athletes), fierce competitiveness. The best of the glider pilots is aware of incipient lift that others don't notice, knows at what speed to fly, in what direction to head, when to circle to gain altitude, and when to leave a thermal in search of a better one. The top glider pilots, like top athletes, have star power. They know each other and are known to the soaring fraternity. They consistently outperform us mortals.

And for us mortals, the chance to keep getting a little better and better is one of the attractions of the sport.

Profile

Al Santilli

Photo courtesy of Al Santilli

l Santilli doesn't like power planes. He is afraid of them. They have engines that can quit. He prefers gliders, and has spent 6,000 happy hours in them.

Al acknowledges that glider flying is more of a challenge than power flying, but he argues that it's less risky. To be sure, he had to bail out of a glider once, but in his scale of scares, that doesn't measure up to the time he unknowingly flew a Piper Cub Special with a broken engine from Hobbs, New Mexico to Albuquerque. That was in the fall of 1947, when he was 33. He was in the Army at the time, based in Albuquerque, and he was flying both gliders and power planes in his spare time.

Like most pilots, he looked for excuses to fly, and one weekend decided to use a PA-11 (aka Piper Cub Special) that he and three other men owned to visit a soaring friend in Hobbs, three hundred miles away. With its beefy 90-horsepower engine, the PA-11 cruised at 100 mph, a big step up from the original Cub. On the way south to Hobbs on Saturday, Al probably fueled up at Roswell. On the way back the next day, because of deteriorating weather and the limited amount of daylight still left, he bypassed Roswell, flying nonstop to Albuquerque. He tied down the plane and went home.

The next morning, Al had a phone call from Al Fiedler, a mechanic at the airfield. "Santilli," he said, "what did you do to that airplane?"

"Nothing," said Al. "I just shut it down and went home."

"Well," said Fiedler, "I can't turn the propeller. It's frozen." Al checked with his co-owners and then told Fiedler to fix it if he could. After Fiedler dug into the problem, he found that in one of the two magnetos (the devices that fire the pairs of spark plugs in each cylinder), a spacer to keep ball bearings aligned had disintegrated. So long as the engine kept running, the ball bearings stayed in their track and did their job. When the engine was stopped, the ball bearings fell into a heap, the teeth on a drive gear jammed, and nothing would turn.

Al was shaken up by this experience. Between Roswell and Albuquerque there's a lot of rugged terrain. "I got pretty close on that one," he told me. "Since that particular experience I haven't built up much time in power planes." Al had logged about 250 hours in power planes before that flight to Hobbs. If now asked his total time in power planes, he says "about 250 hours." Actually, although he dedicated his life to soaring after that, he did log another twenty or so hours in power planes. His PA-11, he said, "ran like a top" once it was fixed, and the next spring he took Lois, his wife-to-be, up in it to fly over Mount Taylor, a beautiful isolated mountain in west central New Mexico (one of the Navajo's sacred mountains) that rises to an altitude of 11,300 feet and is snow-capped much of the year. Al declines to speculate on whether that flight advanced his courtship. I suspect it did.

Now about that bail-out. It happened not long after the Hobbs-to-Albuquerque flight that so unnerved Al. He was making his second flight in a glider he had just purchased from a pair of Army sergeants. The first flight had gone without incident. Before the second flight, meticulous as always, Al checked the glider and found nothing amiss. But right away during the tow, he realized that something was wrong. He heard a snapping noise, and found that he could move the stick fore and aft several inches with no response from the elevator. It wasn't easy to stay in position behind the tow plane. Here's Al's description of what happened: "I nursed it as far as I could on tow till I got high enough. After I released, it was still unmanageable so I jettisoned the canopy and jumped out and here I am talking to you. I landed near Ken Schultz's Buick place."

Al surmised afterward that the glider's elevator may have suffered more stress than it could take on its trip by land to Albuquerque. The sergeants had towed it behind a car on an open trailer with the elevator clamped but exposed. Al figured they had been driving at 50 mph or more into a fierce headwind, subjecting the glider to a gale of 80 mph or so. The poor elevator couldn't quite take it.

"Do you always wear a parachute when flying a glider?" I asked Al. "Yeah, absolutely, I do," he answered, "except when instructing or examining candidates for a license." (When Al examined me, and when he gave me a little extra instruction later, neither of us wore parachutes.)

Al hasn't had to use a parachute since that time, more than sixty years ago, when he floated down toward Ken Schultz's Buick place. But he's come close. What worries most glider pilots even more than a glider coming unglued in flight is a mid-air collision. On a good day near a gliderport, the sky can be full, some gliders being towed out, some approaching to land, and some circling in close proximity to one another as they share a thermal. Vigilance is needed. Al has never had a mid-air collision, but he has kept count of the near misses, and can recite the details of all seven of them. Five occurred near Moriarty, New Mexico, home of the Albuquerque Soaring Club; one near Hutchinson, Kansas; and one near Elmira, New York. "As I discovered by talking to the other pilots afterwards," Al told me, "none of them saw me. I fly defensively, and I was lucky. I just happened to see 'em in time."

Now in his nineties, Al is still flying. When I talked to him in the fall of 2005, he said, almost apologetically, that it had been two weeks since his last flight. Coping with his wife's recent death, he explained, and his move into a new apartment, had been occupying his time. But he hoped to get back into the swing of things, as he put it. "And, just the day before yesterday, I buttoned up my Libelle [his present glider, a high-performance ship imported from Germany] after dismantling all the inspection ports and having it re-examined for another annual inspection. It is fit to fly." Whether Al is the oldest active pilot I haven't been able to determine. There are no official records of such things. My unofficial inquiries suggest that as of 2006 there were no more than two or three nonagenarians still boring holes in the sky as "pilots in command."

Al Santilli was born in Providence, Rhode Island in 1914, the only child of Camillo and Maria Bridget Louise (Mary) Santilli, both immigrants from Isernia, Italy. Camillo came first; Mary followed. Camillo, because he was a mechanic, was exempt from the draft in World War I, but in 1918, when Al was four, he contracted influenza and was disabled for the rest of his life, with seriously damaged eyesight. Al's mother Mary became a seamstress and draperer, and money was always tight in the Santilli household. Al earned his own way from a young age.

Al learned Italian before he learned English, but he had mastered English pretty well by the time he entered kindergarten (Providence was ahead of its time with required kindergarten). His playmates were mostly from immigrant families, too, but from various countries with various languages, so English became the common currency for this bunch of kids.

Al is small in stature. Even in grade school, most of his fellow students towered over him. "I learned to watch out for the bullies," he told me. "Size was the governing factor. But I could run fast, and they didn't catch me. That was one of my concerns when I was growing up." One thing not of concern to Al in school was academics. He excelled in his classes. In high school, chemistry and physics were his favorite subjects. He started flying gliders in the tenth grade, and by the time he was a senior, he began to see the links between science and soaring. "The whole thing was so fascinating I couldn't learn fast enough," he said.

How did an impoverished lad from the immigrant community get into soaring? It started with a chance encounter with a Jenny, a World War I biplane. Al, still in grade school, had been taken by his parents to a farm near Providence, where they were in search of an inexpensive supply of milk. There, in the farmer's field, sat the Jenny. While his parents were talking to the farmer, Al, enthralled with the airplane, was chinning himself on one of the metal hoops below the Jenny's lower wing, mounted there to keep the wing from dragging the ground. The Jenny's pilot, instead of shooing Al away, picked him up and sat him in the pilot's seat. Looking back on that first encounter with an airplane, Al said, "I decided then and there I was going to fly. Every time an airplane would come by I'd listen for its drone."

In high school, Al made model gliders and model airplanes (the latter with rubber-band power) and flew them competitively. The Providence Journal sponsored model-plane contests and featured some of Al's best-performing models in its pages. As he said later, "That was quite a motivation. And one of the best things," he added, "was competing in Boston, forty miles to the north. One of my heartbreaks," he added, "was to lose a 36-inch-span twin pusher model that went down in Boston Harbor. But I had brought spare material. I stayed up all night to make a replacement model and competed the next day."

In 1930, at sixteen and in the tenth grade, Al found a way to fly real gliders. The adult son of a local minister got interested in flying, bought two gliders, and formed a soaring club in Providence. Al was first in line. He didn't have much money but he had gumption. "I went to the neighbors and to local businesses: 'Can I do something for you this week?' And I went to the airfield and offered to do any kind of work that they wanted: coiling ropes, splicing ropes, and all that." When he was a high-school senior, a representative of the U.S. Commerce Department (responsible for aviation) came to the glider field and said to Al, "Hey, kid, do you know that you've got to have a license to fly that thing?" So Al got a learner's permit, belatedly, and before long a private glider license.

In the summer of 1932, after graduating from high school and before enrolling in Brown University as an engineering major, Al went to what was then the nation's premier soaring center, Elmira, New York, and competed, winning a cup for reaching the second highest altitude in the event. His stellar high-school record got him into Brown with scholarships and loans. He was so eager to finish his education that he didn't take a job on the outside. He just let his debts build up. But financial exigencies did not get in the way of his passion for soaring. "I couldn't devote much money to gliding," he told me, "but I did devote quite a bit of time to it. It was during my undergraduate years that I got some hands-on experience repairing gliders." Following his college graduation (cum laude) he also started flying power planes and got his license in a Piper Cub.

Between his 1936 graduation from Brown and his induction into the Army in 1942, Al worked as an electrical engineer, first on radios and prototype televisions for Philco, then on instruments—especially weather instruments—for Karl Otto Heinrich Lange, a Harvard professor who had a business on the side (not a new phenomenon). In his soaring activities, he got as far afield as Wichita Falls, Texas, where he made his first lengthy cross-country flights. It was in Michigan in 1939 or 1940 that he did his only damage to a glider (not counting the one that later came unsprung in flight over Albuquerque and precipitated the parachute jump). Al was flying a primitive glider that had no spoilers to steepen his descent and no shock absorber on the single wheel. He didn't recover quickly enough from a slip on the approach to landing and touched down hard. "I stopped," Al told me, "came to a halt very nicely, did not overrun the landing area, and saw the grass looking at me between my feet and the rudder pedals."

*S*hortly after Pearl Harbor, Al submitted a proposal for an automated weather station to be located in Trinidad, to help in antisubmarine warfare. He was forthwith invited down to Ft. Monmouth in New Jersey for an interview. The interviewing officer, a Colonel Mayer, said, "Santilli, you're wasting your time where you are right now. Are you registered for the draft?" Al said that he was. "Well," said Colonel Mayer, "don't do anything. If you get called, get in touch with me. I can't tell you anything more."

"Lo and behold," Al told me, "within a very short period of time I got a telegram. 'Second Lieutenant Santilli report for duty at Ft. Monmouth.'"

As it turned out, Al spent twenty-three years in the Army. Except when he was in the South Pacific in World War II and at NATO headquarters in Europe after the war, he didn't let it interfere with his soaring. His assignment to Albuquerque in 1947 was fortuitous, placing him right in the middle of some of the country's finest soaring conditions. He married Lois in Albuquerque in 1952, and, after his discharge in 1965, he stayed. His wife's death came after fifty-three years of marriage. He's just getting used to living alone.

*A*l joined the Albuquerque Soaring Club in 1965 and is still an active member, having served as its president twice, its treasurer at least once, and, of course, its resident instructor and examiner. He is also the unofficial teacher, lecturer, and mentor for all the other pilots in his orbit, regardless of their experience. His knowledge of weather, soaring lore, and soaring technique is seemingly limitless. He can lecture on any subject until his audience, be it one person or several, begins to nod off. I, for one, thought until very recently that Al was trained as a professional meteorologist, since there didn't seem to be anything about weather he didn't know (and wasn't willing to impart).

As with so much else in soaring, there are amateur practitioners (such as me) and professionals (such as Al Santilli). Through disquisitions to anyone willing to listen, Al does his best to turn the amateurs into professionals.

Al Santilli died on June 25, 2007, at the age of 93, a few weeks after this book was published. He flew until shortly before his death.

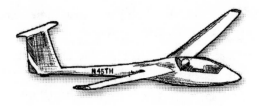

- 4 -

The Landing

*A*t five minutes past seven in the evening on July 1, 1996, I was three thousand feet above Nevada's Minden-Tahoe Airport, nestled in the single-seat cockpit of glider N45TH, almost exactly where I had been seven hours earlier after releasing from a tow plane and setting out to fly five hundred kilometers without an engine. That's roughly the straight-line distance from Boston to Baltimore or Cleveland to Chicago, a bit more than Phoenix to San Diego. I was savoring victory. I had piloted the Rolladen-Schneider* LS-4 from Minden to Tinnemaha Dam in the Owens Valley south of Bishop, California, and back, a round-trip distance by great-circle reckoning of 511 kilometers, or 317 miles. I estimate that if my glider had been equipped with an odometer keeping track of my passage through the air, with all the twists and turns and circles, it would have recorded

---

* Like many of the finest gliders, made in Germany.

about 700 miles that afternoon. But to the Soaring Society of America (of Hobbs, New Mexico) and the Fédération Aéronautique Internationale (of Lausanne, Switzerland), only the great-circle distance matters. I had, at last, completed a task—the second of three—that would add to my quest for a diamond soaring badge.

These certifying organizations also take no interest in total vertical travel. To get from one place to another in a glider, you actually spend most of your time going up or going down. During the course of the afternoon, I had probably climbed more than 60,000 feet and descended an equal distance. So add twenty to twenty-five miles of vertical travel to my 700 miles of horizontal travel.

My first effort to fly a glider 500 kilometers had been in 1982, when I made it from Moriarty, New Mexico to a pasture in White Deer, Texas, a distance of 440 kilometers (275 miles). There, for the first and last time, I damaged a glider in landing, thanks to a culvert overgrown with grass that looked every bit like smooth ground from the air. I touched down just short of the culvert and came to an all-too-abrupt stop as the glider's nose encountered the far side of the culvert. Thanks to shoulder belts as well as a lap belt, my psyche was the only part of me that was bruised, and damage to the glider was fortunately minor.

Other efforts had followed, in Arizona and in Nevada. Some of these flights ended back at the departure airport when rational thought told me that I still had a chance to get home but had no chance to make the targeted distance. Some ended at other airports, often untended. At a paved landing strip in Green Valley, Arizona, a motorist drove up to see if I was all right after watching what appeared to be (and was) an exciting landing in a turbulent crosswind at the fringe of a thunderstorm. Fortunately, I pulled it off and even touched down gently. At a crop-duster's dirt strip in Ak Chin, Arizona, I hailed a pickup truck that happened by and was taken to a telephone. At Luke Air Force Base #1, an abandoned military field northwest of Phoenix where weeds were waving their green wands through cracks in the macadam, an officer who was overseeing rope descents from helicopters was kind enough to drive me to a nearby bar/hamburger joint—after first dressing me down for landing without authorization on government property. He calmed down when I pointed out that with the sun low in the sky, the lift all gone, and no engine to help me, I really did not have the option of landing on non-government property. At a little-used Marine Corps dirt strip in Sweetwater, Nevada, I was able to make radio contact with another glider pilot—one still aloft. He relayed to home base my request for a tow plane to come and pull me out.

The landing in the White Deer, Texas pasture wasn't the only one of my "outlandings" where the ground was too rough or the space too tight to permit being towed back into the air. As a general rule, a tow plane can come and retrieve a glider only if the glider has landed at an airport or on an airstrip intended for power planes. Occasionally, an open field may be large enough and smooth enough to permit the tow plane to come in and tow the glider out, but normally when a glider ends up in the boondocks, it must be disassembled and its wings, tail, and body placed carefully in a special trailer, usually one designed specifically for the particular glider. It is then towed home by car or truck and reassembled. This is not as miserable an experience as you might think. Every glider is designed for just such an eventuality, and the disassembly and reassembly go quickly, at least if handled by two or more people.

On my flight to White Deer (toward an intended target farther east in Oklahoma), my friend Kalman Oravecz provided support. He had flown gliders in Hungary before moving to a faculty position at New Mexico Tech. Kalman dreamed of flying again, and just to feel a part of the adventure, he drove a pickup a hundred miles from Socorro to Moriarty, then continued nearly three hundred more miles pulling a trailer for the glider I was flying, a Schweizer 1-26 (made in America). He and I met up with the help of a previously agreed-on communication link. I was to call the Flight Service Station in Amarillo, Texas, by radio if possible, otherwise by phone after landing, letting the government servants at the Station know my whereabouts. I called from the ground. The Flight Service people, friendly as usual, and curious about my little exploit, let Kalman know where I was when he checked in with them late in the afternoon. By the time we met up in White Deer and got the glider taken apart and put into its trailer, it was after dark. Then we had a good dinner, found a motel, and headed back to Moriarty, New Mexico the next day.

Once, at a ranch in New Mexico, I landed on grazing land, picking a spot within half a mile or so of the ranch house so that I could walk there and phone for help. I was greeted at the door by a beefy rancher who, after hearing my story, asked, suspiciously, "Did you hit a cow?" Only when I assured him that I had not did he unblock the door and invite me in to use the phone. On still another occasion in New Mexico, I landed in an entrancingly lovely and smooth field of wild flowers, remote from habitation. A few hours later, well after dark, I was walking northward along a dirt road in the general direction of the town of Mountainair, when a vehicle finally came along. The driver stopped when I hailed him. It turned out to be the Sheriff, out looking for me.

No one would have to look for me this time. Using the standard glider frequency of 123.3 megahertz, I called the Soar Minden office and reported my altitude and location.* Tony Sabino, Soar Minden's owner and manager, came right back on the radio: "Tango Hotel [his shorthand for my call sign, N45TH], the gear handle is the one in front of you on the upper left." In other words: Quit fooling around. Lower the

---

* Most aircraft communications channels lie between 118 and 136 megahertz (MHz), a seemingly small slice of the radio spectrum, but one into which more than 700 voice channels are now crammed. This slice lies somewhere between the high end of the FM radio band (108 MHz) and TV Channel 7 (174-180 MHz). Most of the assigned aircraft frequencies are specific to a particular location, such as an airport control tower, but a few are more "generic," being available for a particular kind of communication nationwide, such as glider pilots talking to one another or to a ground station.

landing gear and get on down here. In my euphoric state, I was in no hurry to stop flying, but I followed Tony's advice. At a quarter past seven, I rolled off the runway on the glider's single wheel to a smooth stop in the staging area and lowered my left wing to the pavement—one of my better landing performances, executed before an audience of half a dozen people awaiting my arrival. There was Tony, hand-held radio in one hand and a bottle of champagne in the other, together with some fellow pilots, a few of whom had attempted distance flights that day. I turned off the radio and the battery switch in the glider, closed the valve that linked an oxygen tank in the back of the glider to a face mask I had been using on and off during the day, raised my bubble canopy, and accepted a plastic cup of champagne while someone snapped a picture of my broad smile. Tony was not one to waste good champagne pouring it over a pilot's head, which was fine with me. I half suspected that he had a way of reintroducing fizz so that he could use one bottle several times. I learned later that the photo of my grinning face just after landing proved useful. Tony showed it at one or more promotional talks he gave to prove that even a seventy-year old couldn't miss with Soar Minden's equipment and guidance. (He added the flourish that my 500-kilometer flight occurred on my seventieth birthday, a statement within a couple of months of being true.)

"Yours was the only successful distance flight today," said Tony, raising his glass. "The blue thermals defeated the rest." It was a dry day, one in which "blue thermals" predominated until late in the day. A blue thermal is a rising column of air that is not topped by a cloud, so nothing marks its presence. It can be found only by chance or good guessing. On a not-quite-so-dry day, small cumulus clouds sit atop thermals, making them easier to find.

As I was unfastening my harness and starting to clamber from the cockpit while accepting the congratulations of the assembled welcoming party, it came to me that my last bathroom visit had been eight hours ago. "Excuse me," I said, "I need a pit stop." As I made my way to the small terminal building to take care of that need, others rolled my glider to its resting space and tied it down. I returned to it to remove two water bottles, an empty packet of Peanut M&M's, an unopened package of cheese crackers, a microphone, the oxygen gear, a map, a sweater and jacket (for the possibility of spending the night in the desert), and the all-important camera and recording barograph.

A recording barograph of the kind I used contains a soot-coated piece of tinfoil wrapped on a small cylinder against which the sharp tip of a pen rests. As the cylinder slowly rotates (once around every four hours), the pen, actuated by air pressure, makes a running record of the glider's altitude. This seemingly crude device is surprisingly accurate, once it is tested in a low-pressure chamber and certified. On my flight it served two purposes— to show that I made no intermediate landings and to show that I did not exceed my legal limit of 18,000 feet above sea level. (Among a glider pilot's nagging worries is forgetting to turn on the barograph before takeoff. To avoid the awful embarrassment of completing a flight for which a record is needed and discovering that there is no record, the pilot includes in his pre-takeoff check list, "Listen for the ticking of the barograph"—or the equivalent cautionary phrase if the flight record is to be made by an electronic GPS unit.) In the United States, no one can legally venture above 18,000 feet unless in contact with and following the instructions of controllers on the ground. At their discretion, controllers can make an exception to this rule by opening temporary "wave windows" for gliders. A wave window is a chunk of airspace maybe ten miles by ten miles in size and extending up to some altitude chosen by the controllers—say 25,000 or 30,000 feet, or even unlimited. Within this confined space, glider pilots can venture as high as they are able without any moment-to-moment communication with the ground, while the controllers route powered aircraft around the window.

There were no such windows for my flight, so I had to stay under 18,000 feet. It wasn't easy. In a glider, altitude is money in the bank—the more of it you have, the more numerous your options and the better your chance of going where you want to go. If you are riding a thermal up through 16,000 and 17,000 feet as I did several times that day, it takes willpower to leave the thermal and move on (and down) when the altimeter edges toward 18,000. I exercised that willpower three times at 17,800. Tony, examining and measuring the barograph record that evening, claimed that I had busted 18,000 at least once. "Not according to my altimeter," I said. Fortunately, the powers that judge these matters decided that my apparent infraction was within the limits of uncertainty of the device.

A camera is used to prove that the pilot reached the claimed turn point, in my case Tinnemaha Dam. The camera, mounted rigidly on the left side of the canopy, looks outward along the left wing. This means that I had to be making a left turn south of the dam as I snapped the picture (actually, several pictures, just to be sure). It means, too, that the left turn should be banked steeply, say about 60 degrees. To catch a view of the dam in a shallower bank would require flying farther past it before turning and thus wasting time and miles. Tony, my official observer, had to load the film in the camera, close it with wire and a lead seal, reopen it upon my return, and supervise the development of the film. You wouldn't think that there are cheats in the sport of soaring, but maybe there are. The certifying organizations are careful.

A glider pilot who wants to do more than linger in a thermal near home base on a Sunday afternoon performs tasks and earns badges. The A, B, and C badges recognize basic skills. Then—with ascending challenge—come the bronze, silver, gold, and diamond badges (followed, for a few, by the 1,000-kilometer diplome*). The three achievements needed for the diamond badge are a flight of at least 300 kilometers over a closed course that has been designated in advance; a flight of at least 500 kilometers, which need not be closed and need not be designated in advance; and a flight that includes an altitude gain of 5,000 meters, or 16,400 feet. I had

---

* Yes, diplome, not diploma. French is the language of the awarding organization.

completed a 300-kilometer diamond triangle in New Mexico back in 1980, and my diamond altitude flight was nearly three years in the future. It came on March 27, 1999. I released from one of Tony Sabino's tow planes at around 10,000 feet above sea level, dropped to 9,500 feet while probing for lift, and then rode a mountain wave* to a little over 27,000 feet, from where I got a spectacular view of Lake Tahoe and the Sierras, in relative comfort in my heavy flight suit, gloves, wool socks, and boots. (It's cold up there and gliders have no heaters.) I earned, finally, diamond Badge Number 858 in the United States, Number 6343 in the world.

---

* A mountain wave is undulating air generated by wind over a mountain range. I'll discuss this kind of lift in Chapter 5. It can extend far higher than the mountain tops.

$\mathcal{P}$ rofi$\mathcal{l}$e

Tony Sabino

Photo courtesy of Tony Sabino

When an elderly man in a suit walks into the office of Soar Minden at the Minden-Tahoe Airport in Nevada, what Tony Sabino sees is a wallet. When an impecunious young flyer walks in, what Tony sees is someone in need of cheap housing, a free meal, and the loan of a car. In both cases, he responds accordingly.

Tony has been the owner and manager of Soar Minden since 1988, and has kept it afloat—or aloft—all that time, against a not-always-friendly airport management and in the face of competition from another soaring operation on the field (an operation that folded in 2004). He is hard-nosed businessman and benevolent father-figure rolled into one.

The young and the old, the well-off and the not-so-well-off, the Japanese and Europeans and Americans, all in search of good soaring, keep coming back to Soar Minden—I among them. Tony provides good gliders (or sailplanes, as we like to call them) as well as a helpful array of extras, such as parachutes, gloves, fleece-lined boots, barographs, oxygen masks—and advice. He encourages adventurous flying and he gets you into the air without a lot of standing around. It helps that Soar Minden—possibly the largest and most successful commercial glider operation in the world—is located in fabulous soaring country. Tony advertises 360 days per year of soarable weather, and that's pretty close to the truth. The sun and the desert contribute strong thermals. The nearby Sierras contribute strong waves (see Chapter 5).

As of 2006, fifteen years after he took over personal management of Soar Minden (he was owner and overseer in absentia for a couple of years before that), Tony's inventory consisted of a dozen gliders, five tow planes (four in service and one being overhauled), and eight golf carts—plus a meter-maid cart. His average number of customer glider flights per year is about 5,000. He describes his business as about one-third American pilots, one-third foreign pilots, and one-third scenic rides for non-pilots. His annual cash flow is around three-quarters of a million dollars (including fuel sales for what he calls planes with whirly things on their front ends). If he has a financial officer or business manager to keep track of it, it isn't obvious. He is, as the saying goes, a hands-on manager.

Before taking over the management of Soar Minden, Tony spent twenty-two years in the military, eleven as an enlisted man in the Air Force and eleven as an officer in the Navy. It all started in 1969, when, in the course of a few months, he dropped out of college (he says he flunked out, but he may be exaggerating), got married, took a job at Bethlehem Steel, and enlisted in the Air Force. The enlistment was his way of avoiding the draft and possible Army service in Vietnam. Although he didn't go to Vietnam, he touched down in a lot of other places: the United Kingdom, Korea, Diego Garcia, and various bases in the United States. It was in the UK that he took up soaring and literally touched down (many times). Later, at Andrews Air Force base in Virginia (home port for Air Force One), he gained his private and commercial glider licenses and his license to fly power planes (the ones with whirly things up front). His last assignment was to the Naval Air Station in Fallon, Nevada, just seventy-five miles from the Minden-Tahoe airport and his target, Soar Minden.

Tony Sabino was born in New York City in 1948, to a mother who was a physician and a father who was in retail sales at Macys. When Tony was just seven, his father treated him to a fifteen-minute seaplane ride around New York. Tony describes it as a memorable experience, but isn't quite willing to say that that's when the flying bug bit. That moment may have come years later during his first months in the Air Force, when he was stationed in England. As he puts it, "While there, casting about for things to do other than drinking beer, I fell in with RAF folk and joined the RAF gliding/soaring association. I learned to fly with the RAF in a club-type atmosphere and I found that very rewarding and very warm and good and I stayed with it for many years."

Stayed with it indeed until the present moment, although it must be said that Tony hardly has time to fly for fun any more. Getting other people into the air and witnessing their achievements is where he now finds reward. Still, over the course of the years, he has spent more than 1,000 hours aloft in gliders—as well as a "couple of hundred" in power planes.

Tony's family moved from New York to New Jersey when he was young and then on to Baltimore, Maryland. In 1966, at the age of seventeen, he graduated from Baltimore Polytechnic Institute (which sounds like a college but is a high school). He spent about two years at the nearby University of Maryland before he "flunked out" and took the life-changing steps mentioned above: marriage, working for a steel company, and joining the Air Force.

In due course—but not pell-mell—Tony fathered three sons, all while he was in the Air Force. The first, Tony (known as A. J.) was born in 1972. Then came Paul in 1976 and Sean in 1977. All three of these boys, when in their teens, worked at Soar Minden, and all three soloed gliders at age 14, which is the earliest legal age to do so. Sean told me that for him working at the airport was a privilege, not a chore. He could fly a glider with an instructor aboard when he was twelve, and had to wait impatiently for his fourteenth birthday to fly alone. Tony paid his sons not in money but in flying time, and this seemed more than fair to the boys

In the Air Force, as a supply and club manager, Tony migrated through the enlisted grades from Airman to Staff Sergeant. In his free time, he diligently flew when he could, and diligently studied when he could. Thanks to the University of Maryland's overseas program, he could take courses both in the United Kingdom and in Korea. After eight years of part-time study, he earned a bachelor's degree in business. In the eyes of the military, this suddenly made him officer material.

Tony chose to cash in this officer potential by transferring to the Navy, where he became an Ensign and eventually a Lieutenant. Such inter-service transfer is not the norm, but Tony managed it. If strings were pulled to make it happen, Tony isn't saying. Paradoxically, by moving from the Air Force to the Navy, he moved closer to aviation, not farther from it. He became an aircraft maintenance officer, in which capacity he was authorized to fly the planes he and his crew serviced, to see if the planes and their instruments performed properly. Not a bad policy. What better motivator for quality and safety than to have the person who supervised an airplane's repair be the first person to fly it? This policy even got Tony into a jet trainer, the T-2 Buckeye.

Checkout flights brought practical rewards for the maintenance officer, too. The officer who flew more than a few hours per month was rewarded with a handsome salary bonus known officially as flight pay, and unofficially as "flight skins."

ike many military officers looking toward retirement while still young, Tony had to give thought to what to do next. Once established in Fallon, Nevada, his last Navy post, he cast an eye toward Minden and took the plunge to buy the Soar Minden operation nearly three years before his retirement from the Navy. He hired a manager until he could take it over personally, and since 1991 it's been his life and his passion. "This is certainly the nicest flying place in the world," Tony told me, "and day for day the best flying place in the world." He meant this remark to encompass both the place and the service he provides. He can be forgiven for saying so. And he may be right.

Indeed all those wonderful soaring conditions wouldn't be much use if there weren't a Soar Minden or similar operation to provide the necessities of flight. Think what is needed just to soar in a wave up to 25,000 or 30,000 feet looking down on the mortals below. Not just a glider and a tow plane to get it launched. Also a barograph, a tank of oxygen, a face mask, a radio and a microphone, a pair of very warm boots and gloves to match, a heavy jacket, a deal with Air Traffic Control to open a wave window, and words of wisdom on what to do if trapped above a cloud or if the oxygen system seems to be malfunctioning. Tony provides all of that.

The radio is not just for chatting. At least for novice pilots, Tony or one of his deputies calls the pilot at high altitude every ten minutes or so, to check for possible hypoxia, or oxygen deprivation. If the pilot responds with slurred speech or illogical statements, or sounds excessively euphoric, or doesn't respond at all, the peremptory command from the ground is, "Hold that mask tight over your face, and get on down here!" At those altitudes, a pilot with no oxygen at all remains conscious for only a few minutes. With some but not enough oxygen, the pilot remains conscious but develops one or more odd symptoms, which someone with Tony's experience can detect from the way the pilot talks. The converse problem, hyperventilation, is not so easy to detect—and is not so serious.

I asked Tony about Soar Minden's safety record. In eighteen years and perhaps 75,000 glider flights, there has been only one fatal crash in one of his gliders. That occurred in April 1997, when a relatively low-time pilot (30 hours in gliders), in his first solo flight in a high-performance ship, jettisoned the glider's canopy—whether accidentally or intentionally no one will ever know—and augered into the ground after apparently being knocked unconscious by the canopy frame as it disengaged. The other serious accident I learned about from Tony occurred in 2005, when one of his customers failed to lock the canopy on his glider. When the canopy popped loose in flight, the pilot crash-landed, destroying the glider he was flying as well as one he landed on top of, and put himself in the hospital for a while.

Of course, Tony's planes are not the only ones flying in the Carson Valley around Minden, and there have been other fatalities there, quite a few of them over the years. In one twelve-month period in 1999-2000, there were three fatal glider crashes near Minden, claiming four lives. The most widely-reported of these involved Donald Engen, 75, a Navy vice admiral and director of the National Air and Space Museum, flying in a motor glider with that plane's owner, William Ivans, 79, a former president of the Soaring Society of America. For unknown reasons, a wing sheared off the plane, and both men were killed in the ensuing crash. ("Motor glider" may sound like a contradiction in terms, but it isn't. Some gliders have small motors that can be run briefly to enable the glider to get launched without the help of a tow plane or can be fired up when a pilot runs out of lift and doesn't care to land on some inhospitable patch of ground. In some motor gliders, the engine's propeller folds neatly inside the fuselage when the motor isn't running, rather like a convertible top tucking itself inside the rear end of a car.)

As to his personal safety record, Tony admits to only one goof-up. He once failed to latch a canopy securely. After it popped open in flight, he landed safely. The glider was damaged, but he wasn't.

A t Soar Minden, Tony is entrepreneur, promoter, hand-holder, and gruff uncle. He personally serves as the official observer for many pilots seeking badges of one kind or another—maybe a hundred in a year. He's worried about the decline in the number of young people taking up soaring. His clientele, like the population in general, is graying.

I asked Tony's friend Sam Whiteside, a glider pilot, glider instructor, and real-estate salesman, what makes Tony tick. "Who knows?" he answered. "He has to run a business. Some customers find him incredibly annoy-ing. Others find him incredibly gracious. One thing's for sure. He is never mean." Tony's second wife, Kathleen (who died of cancer in 2005) was an important part of the gracious side, Sam told me. "She hosted dinners and helped out many of the pilots, especially the young and not-so-wealthy ones from overseas."

I told Sam my own assessment of Tony: abrasive but lovable. "That's about it," said Sam. "The abrasive part is his business side. The lovable part is the real Tony."

-5-

From A to B

t the beginning of my flying career, when I was scooting around the Midwest in my little Ercoupe, and at the end of my flying career, when I was trying to cover ground in a glider, I used the same method of navigation: a finger on a map. The government provided (and still provides) maps called Sectional Charts that show the towns, road, lakes, railroads, and rivers more or less as they appear from the air. Back in 1954, if I was planning to fly, let's say, from Bloomington, Indiana, to Decatur, Illinois, I drew a straight line connecting those two cities (more exactly, connecting their airports) on a Sectional Chart, then made little tick marks every ten miles along this line. (I had a handy ruler scaled for the chart.) I knew that at my plane's speed of 100 miles per hour, it would take six minutes from one tick mark to the next in the absence of wind. With a brisk tailwind of 20 knots, it would take five minutes. Flying into a 20-knot headwind, it would take seven-and-a-half minutes. So, once established on my route, I would pencil in the time that I passed a tick mark and the estimated time when I would reach the next one. When I got to the next one, I could see whether I was a bit ahead of or behind schedule, and thus whether I was estimating the wind correctly. If I got a bit confused and couldn't identify a particular point under a tick mark because everything on the ground looked more or less the same, I would just keep going in the same direction and identify my location at the next tick mark. The method worked fine. It was said in those days that if a pilot could find the way to a point ten miles from the home airport, he (or she) could fly anywhere. It was true. (Out west, it can be easier. You take a bead on a mountain fifty miles away and fly toward it. I remember years later, in flying from Socorro to Denver via Alamosa, Colorado, I had radio navigation equipment aboard, but hardly needed it. From thirty miles south of Alamosa, I could see the little round white house that held the radio beacon and used my eyes instead of my radio to fly right toward and over it.)

In a glider flight, it's still finger-on-the-map navigation, but the line and the tick marks serve a different function. The line is certainly not a path that can be followed. It's more like a long arrow pointing to your destination, serving to remind you how far off a direct route you are as you weave and circle toward your goal. The tick marks play a safety role. They help you figure out how far you can glide from whatever altitude you're at if you run out of lift. Suppose, for example, that you are flying a glider with a lift-to-drag ratio of 40. This means that under ideal conditions in still air, and flown at the right speed, it will fly forty miles forward for one mile (about 5,000 feet) of descent. To be conservative, allowing that you might not fly at just the right speed, that squashed bugs on your wing might reduce the glide performance below its advertised value, and that you might encounter down drafts, you decide to base your estimate of how far you can glide on a twenty-to-one instead of a forty-to-one ratio. Then you figure that in twenty miles, you are unlikely to descend more than a mile. So if you are 6,000 feet above an airport that is twenty miles ahead, you are in pretty good shape. Even without any significant bur-bles of lift along the way, and with judicious porpoising, you should arrive over the airport at least 1,000 feet above the ground (having descended 5,000 feet in twenty miles). Having a way out is always on the glider pilot's mind, and when the air doesn't cooperate with your plan-ning, that "way out" may be a pasture, not an airport.

Navigating by radio is completely different, and quite satisfying in its own way. It's office work. Just you and the instruments in a confined space. Your world is the cockpit. What you, the pilot, are trying to do is make those instruments do exactly what you want them to do. It is only incidental that you are in an airplane that is moving through the air. You feel—at least I always felt— that you are controlling the instruments, not controlling an airplane. If, for instance, my altimeter read 5,900 feet when it should have read 6,000 feet, I didn't feel that my job was to move the airplane back up a hundred feet. It was to make the altimeter needle move back to 6,000 feet, to restore that needle to its proper position. A gentle tug back on the wheel or a slight rotation of the trim knob accomplished that result. To me an especially rewarding flight was one in which I disappeared into the mist moments after takeoff and emerged from the mist an hour or two later to see a runway stretched out ahead of me a few hundred feet below. It was a bit like time travel. The world contracted, and when the world expanded, I was somewhere else.

In the dark ages of radio navigation, there was the A-N beacon, now thankfully interred. It made even seasoned airline pilots curse their fate. It used a low-frequency radio signal (below the AM radio band) to guide planes to an airport or a point near an airport. You navigated not by looking at a display on your instrument panel but by listening to scratchy, staticky sounds on your earphones. If you heard a steady tone, you were on course. If you heard the repeated dot-dash of the Morse Code letter A, you were off course on one side. If you heard the repeated dash-dot of the Morse Code letter N, you were off course on the other side. If you were just a *little* off course, you heard the A or the N barely audible over a background roar. The electronic trick was to have the transmitted A's and N's mesh perfectly, each filling in the blanks of the other, along a narrow slice of directions, with the A's or the N's being stronger in other directions. A series of A's is - — - — - — , etc. A series of N's is — - — - — - , etc. You can see that if you superimpose a series of N's on top of a series of A's with just the right timing, you get ————————— , a steady tone.

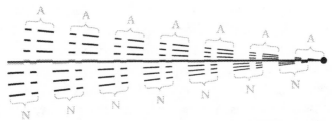

Suffice it to say that not a pilot alive mourns the passing of the A-N beacon. Still, it was better than looking out the window on a dark night and hoping to see some lights below, which is what Lindbergh and his fellow airmail pilots had to do in the 1920s.

Then came the very-high-frequency omni-ranges, the VORs, which are still in service. (It was a VOR station that sat within the small, round white building that let me navigate to Alamosa by eye.) Nowadays a pilot dials in the digital frequency of a VOR station (not far above the FM radio band). Gauges on the instrument panel then obligingly reveal the pilot's distance and direction from the station. In the early days, it was only the direction, not the distance, that was available, and the frequency was found by a kind of trial and error using a "coffee grinder" radio. The pilot turned a knob that caused an indicator to slide across a radio dial as the signals of different stations faded in and out. Upon hearing the call sign of the desired VOR station, the pilot gently twiddled the dial back and forth to optimize the signal, just as my grandfather did to get the best reception of The Lone Ranger.

Now the VOR, even with its digital magic, is becoming obsolete, as the Global Positioning System (GPS) takes over as the primary means of navigation. (Only in the final stages of approach for landing are radio aids still important.) GPS, now common in cars and boats and in hand-held units used by hikers, is familiar to many people other than pilots. Talk about digital magic? We take GPS for granted, but its operation depends on the latest in electronic and satellite technology, and even makes practical use of special and general relativity. If only Einstein had lived to see it.

Even glider pilots are taking their fingers off the map as GPS units enter their cockpits. Since a glider has no engine turning a generator to keep a battery charged, the number of electronic gadgets that a glider can accommodate is limited by the ability of a battery to keep it all going for many hours. Fortunately, those gadgets get smaller and smaller and less and less thirsty for electric power, so the glider pilot can talk and navigate all day without fearing that it will all go dead. One big edge that GPS gives a glider pilot in competition is the ability to shave off distance at designated turn points. Without GPS, the pilot must fly far enough past a turn point to wheel around in a steep bank and take a picture of the point, to verify that the corner hasn't been cut. With GPS, the turn can be made closer to the point, with the GPS unit dutifully recording the track to provide later evidence that the pilot didn't cut the corner. GPS accuracy is measured in meters, not kilometers.

I n a glider, it's little help to know where you are if you can't get where you'd like to go. Lift is everything. On a good day—a day with thermals popping up all over—it's no great trick to stay up in one area. The challenge, even on a good day, is to go somewhere, to get from A to B. Usually, this necessarily requires flying through a good deal of air that is going down, not up.

Broadly, there are three kinds of lift. Two if by wind and one if by sun, so to speak. If wind near the ground encounters an upslope, it is swept upward. This is called ridge lift. You can see it at the seashore when an onshore breeze is pushed upward by a sand dune near the beach, allowing gulls to glide back and forth without flapping their wings. In Pennsylvania and extending on down into West Virginia and Tennessee there are ridges hundreds of miles long running from northeast to southwest. When the wind is right—strong and from the northwest—These ridges produce lift that can keep glider pilots aloft all day, if they have the endurance for it. The region is known as the world's longest diamond mine because its ridge lift enables glider pilots to cruise more than five-hundred kilometers—"diamond distance"—often at strikingly high speed. Ridge flights of twice that distance have in fact been accomplished.* I have never done this kind of soaring but I admire the pilots who do. It entails flying a few hundred feet above the trees in turbulent air hour after hour, vigilant every second for changes in wind or

---

* Flights in mountain-generated wave have gone even farther. As of 2006, the world's record distance flight in a glider, set in Argentina in 2004, was 2,192.9 kilometers (1,362.6 miles).

updraft, alert every moment for the possibility of having to turn aside and land in a nearby valley.

Once in Chamonix, France, I had the pleasure of watching a more relaxed kind of ridge soaring. Pilots (or maybe they should be called jumpers), hanging from a kind of rectangular parachute called a paraglider, leapt from the top of a high cliff and glided down toward the valley below. Sometimes, catching ridge lift, they soared back and forth like hawks, remaining aloft, even ascending.

Another kind of wind-generated lift is the mountain wave. It is very distinct from ridge lift because it can extend tens of thousands of feet above the ground. A wave is set up when the wind is blowing briskly across a mountain range and the speed of the wind increases as the altitude increases. When this "gradient" exists, the air downwind from the mountains can undulate up and down in a wave action that has enabled some record-breaking glider flights to more than 40,000 feet. (The record is 49,000 feet. My own highest wave flight went to 27,200 feet. That was exciting enough—and cold enough.) The only visible mark of a mountain wave is a possible "lenticular" cloud, formed when moisture in the air condenses into droplets as the air is cooled by its rising motion in the wave. Lenticular clouds differ from ordinary clouds in that they sit still over a location on the ground, rather than moving with the wind. Pilots use waves mainly to reach for high altitude, but sometimes use them to get from A to B.

It's a common misconception that wind is always needed for lift. Not so. The lift that glider pilots are most familiar with is thermal lift, generated by the sun whether there is wind or not. On a sunny summer morning, the sun goes about its business of heating the earth. Inevitably some spots will be heated more than others—a gravel pit more than a grass field, for instance. This means that the air near the ground is also unevenly heated. Hot air rises. Cooler air falls. This bubbling near the surface leads at first just to light breezes and mild turbulence. But along about late morning or midday, something major happens. Here and there the air over a warm patch of ground rises more forcefully, drawing surrounding air into itself and gaining a life of its own. This thermal column may extend upward a thousand feet or so as it starts to flex its muscles, and later in the day on up to ten thousand feet or more. It may be a few hundred feet across or more than half a mile. It can live for hours and will move with the wind far from where it was triggered. (Thus the pilot cruising over a gravel pit in search of lift may find nothing there. The thermal triggered at that spot could be long gone.)

Like a child who has flown the coop, a thermal, once free of its birthplace, may be large, strong, and independent. A glider pilot circling in a thermal can expect to ascend at a rate of at least 200-300 feet per minute, and perhaps as much as 1,000 feet per minute (the latter rate more likely in the west than the east). If there is enough moisture in the air, a thermal will have a headdress. The rising air cools, the moisture condenses, and a small cumulus cloud forms atop the column. If the top of the cloud looks like a cauliflower, it means that air is still rising within it, creating an uneven upper surface. The glider pilot has a good chance of finding lift under the cauliflower cloud. If the cloud looks more like whipped cream, with a smooth top, it may be the legacy of a thermal that has gone out of business. The glider pilot flying under the whipped cream cloud is likely to be disappointed.

Sometimes thermals can line up shoulder to shoulder to form what is more a wall than a column of lift. The clouds topping the thermals then join into a single "cloud street," a pilot's delight. In a usual columnar thermal, the pilot must circle, sometimes steeply banked, to stay within the zone of lift. The art of thermaling is staying "centered," to take advantage of the strongest lift the thermal has to offer. Under a cloud street, the pilot can cruise along in a straight line, maintaining or gaining altitude without a care in the world—until the cloud street ends.

The principle of soaring cross-country using thermal lift is simple. You gain altitude in a thermal, depart the thermal when its lift weakens or it is about to carry you into its headdress cloud (or into the instrument-control zone above 18,000 feet), then fly straight until you find another thermal, circle in it, and so on. In practice, getting from A to B is not quite so simple. There is the considerable danger that you may not find that next thermal, in which case you will be looking for a suitable place to land. And even if you do succeed in finding one thermal after another, the clock is the enemy. It takes time to gain altitude in a thermal, and the more altitude you lose searching for the next thermal, the more time it takes to regain altitude in it. Even on a good summer day, there may be only six or seven hours of thermal activity, so the question is: How far can you go in that time?

A whole science of cross-country flight using thermals has developed. Back in 1954, the pioneer American glider pilot Paul MacCready (later known for his designs of human-powered and solar-powered aircraft) published the concept of "speed to fly,"* which is the best speed to fly when angling down through sinking air between thermals. Many a glider sports a "MacCready ring" around its airspeed indicator to help the pilot figure out what that optimal speed is. Nowadays a little computer in the cockpit performs the task. The "speed to fly" is counterintuitive because it's faster than you think it should be. If you find yourself in sinking air, your natural tendency is to slow down to the "minimum sink" speed in order not to lose altitude any faster than you have to. But by going faster, you spend less time in the downdraft. And by going *still* faster—by adopting MacCready's "speed to fly"—you minimize the total time you spend going down and then up, which in turn maximizes your average speed over the ground. It's all about getting from A to B.

Several of my unsuccessful efforts to fly a glider 500 kilometers started at Estrella sailport south of Phoenix (es-STRAY-ya if you're a purist, es-STRELL-uh if you're not). Estrella was owned and operated by Les Horvath, a charismatic émigré from Hungary who excelled in both cross-country and aerobatic soaring, and aggressively promoted both in his adopted country. He summed it all up for me one day. "Ken," he said, "When in doubt, fly faster."

---

* He had developed and implemented the idea in 1947-48, sharing it in the pages of *Soaring* magazine in 1954. Preliminary ideas of the same kind date from the 1930s.

$\mathcal{P}rofile$

Les Horvath

Photo courtesy of Les Horvath

$\mathcal{S}$ ome time in late 1967 or early 1968, Les Horvath, who was then 31 and living in upstate New York, called his younger brother Stephan in California, and said, "Stephan, I want to build an airport." Stephan, who, like Les, was an accomplished glider pilot (both had started flying as teens in their native Hungary) didn't hesitate a moment. "Let's do it," he said (or words to that effect). So they agreed that Les would scout in the east and Stephan would scout in the west.

Les and Stephan had done well since getting off the boat in New York eleven years earlier with no money, no contacts, and no English. Les by now had a wife, three children (all boys), a good job, and a nest egg he planned to use, one way or another, to nurture his passion for soaring. Stephan, two years younger, also had a good job, a nest egg, and a family—a wife and two daughters. To Les and Stephan, with brains and confidence to spare,

98

creating a new airport and turning it into a world center for soaring seemed a perfectly reasonable ambition.

In August 1968, Stephan called Les and said, "I have a place I want you to see. Come on out and let's look at it." Over the Labor Day weekend, they got together in Phoenix, and drove out to a spot on government land about 25 miles south of the city. It looked promising. They were confident that abundant sunshine over the desert country would provide good thermal activity pretty much year-round and that the nearby Estrella Mountains, rising more than 3,000 feet above the desert floor, would provide ridge lift, and probably wave activity as well. Although Les had only a student license for power planes at the time, he managed to rent an Aeronca Champ at a suburban airport, and used it to size up the area. When, close to the Estrella Mountains, he encountered a thermal updraft vastly stronger than anything he had ever experienced before, he said, like Brigham Young looking down the west slope of the Wasatch Mountains 121 years earlier, "This is the place."

On April 1, 1969, nine months after first laying eyes on the site, Les and Stephan had leased the needed land from the Federal government, built three runways and an apron, bought two gliders and a tow plane, spread out a big parachute for shade, and were open for business. Here's how Les describes the first customer who showed up that day: "This guy jumps out of his car and he says, 'Here I am. Let's go!' He was an airline pilot from New York City and he read a blurb in *Soaring* magazine that these two Hungarians are going to make an airport southwest of the city of Phoenix and he decided there's only one place it could be—it's gotta be here. So he just took some dirt roads and found us, and he paid for a flight."

Eighteen years later, when Les sold the airport, his inventory consisted of fourteen gliders (including a motor glider), three tow planes, a hangar, an office building, a swimming pool, and two outside johns. He was employing twenty-five people, including an assortment of part-time instructors and tow pilots, and his wife Betty as the office manager. His sons by that time were grown and gone, but they had helped out earlier. Stephan had gone on to other things after about four years in the business, his half being bought out by Les. Les himself stayed on to manage the airport for a couple of more years after he sold it. He could rightfully claim to have built one of the most successful commercial glider ports in the world. (I won't get into the question of Minden vs. Estrella. Both are outstanding soaring centers. Both have provided me with wonderful experiences in the air.)

Les Horvath was born in Budapest, Hungary in 1936, the first of four children. Stephan arrived two years later. Then came another boy and a girl. Les's father worked as a maintenance electrician in a factory. His mother stayed home with the children except when she had to take temporary farm jobs to help make ends meet. Les was a child during World War II and came of age under the Communist dictatorship that followed. It was the unsuccessful revolution in 1956 and the return of the Soviet tanks that triggered his desire to get out. As he put it, "I was supposed to go into the army, and I just wasn't going to be in the Red Army." His implacable hatred of Communism makes him, even now, extremely sensitive to political winds that blow in America.

Les completed eight years of formal education and, at age 14, went to work in his father's factory as an electrician's apprentice, with his father as a boss. He had a friend and neighbor, less financially pressed, who was able to enroll in a two-year electrician's school. When Les turned sixteen, he borrowed the friend's books, studied them for three months, and passed the electrician's exam. With Les bringing in money and his mother supplementing the income a little, the family was getting by, and Stephan was able to stay in school.

At age ten, Les built a radio that worked. At eleven, he fashioned motor-driven machines from heavy paper. A few years later, he and another friend started building model gliders, some sophisticated enough to circle in thermals. The friend designed, Les built. In the spring of 1954 (Les was seventeen), this friend disappeared every weekend. "Finally," says Les, "I caught up with him. I say, 'What's going on?' and he says, 'Next Saturday I'll take you some place and I'll let you see what's going on.' So the next Saturday I went with him and we ended up at the glider port." That shaped the rest of Les's life.

Actually, his first experience in a glider that Saturday scared him to death. He and an instructor were "winched" to an altitude of 700 or 800 feet. (To be "winched" is to be pulled aloft by a long cable attached to a motor-driven winch at the far end of the field.) Once they cut loose from the cable, the instructor showed him that if the stick is moved to one side, the wings tilt and the glider enters a bank. The instructor's draconian method of teaching in a first flight was to allow the bank to continue until the glider was upside down, then to take over the controls, right the ship, and land it. "When we landed," says Les, "I kissed the ground, and I said, 'Never again. This is not for me.' But all week long, the experience was bugging me." The next Saturday, Les was back at the field. A year later, he had accumulated 220 flights, most of them no more than a few minutes in duration, the longest being 45 minutes. In all that time, he had been pulled aloft by a tow plane only once. The other launches were with a winch or a bungee cord.

All this glider training was free, courtesy of the Soviet Air Force. Les had to go to ground school, learn every detail of the glider's construction, learn to pack a parachute, and pass the same rigorous physical exam as a MIG pilot. He was shouted at and hit. It was expected that if he survived the screening process, a MIG pilot is just what he would become. Instead he made his way to America and became one of the world's preeminent glider pilots. He likes to say of motor-driven flight, "I have no use for a power plane other than to get somewhere. It's the same as cars. You turn the key, you go where you want to, you turn the key, and you do what you came to do." By now, Les has logged over 10,000 hours in gliders and about 500 hours in power planes.

With their parent's acquiescence, if not exactly their blessing, Les and Stephan made their way to the Hungarian-Austrian border, leaving Budapest on Sunday, November 18, 1956 for an uncle's house nearer the border, and going on to the border two days later. It was a few weeks after the Soviets had put down the Hungarian revolution and less than a week since the boys decided to leave. Les was twenty, Stephan just shy of eighteen. They said goodbye to their parents and younger siblings, not knowing whether they would be back in a couple of days or never. It turned out to be never. Some friendly border guards accepted a small bribe and they were in Austria. (Les left home with two weeks' salary in his pocket, Stephan with a watch he thought he might sell.)

The Austrians put Les and Stephan and some other border-crossers on a train to Kematen, a small city between Vienna and Salzburg. There, within a couple of weeks, they secured an immigration visa to America and were taken under the wing of Catholic Charities, which temporarily took over the management of these young men's lives—and payment of their bills. With a crowd of other emigrés, they were transported by train from Kematen to Bremerhaven, Germany, and, in a crossing that must have taken about ten days, by ship from there to New York. They arrived in New York on January 16, 1957.

Thanks to Catholic Charities, they were not cast adrift in the big city. They were bussed to Camp Kilmer in New Jersey, where they spent two weeks. Because jobs for electricians were reportedly available in Buffalo, New York, Les and Stephan were put on a bus to that city, where, indeed, Les found work in nearby Lockport. After another week, Stephan, who lacked specific journeyman skills, was placed in a job at a state mental hospital in Poughkeepsie, New York. After about six months, Stephan, by then fluent in English and possessor of a driver's license, took off by car with a friend for California. Les stayed in upstate New York until the brothers rejoined in Arizona nearly a dozen years after their arrival in America.

or years, Les's passion for soaring lay dormant. By the time he joined a soaring club in Utica in 1965, nine years had passed since his arrival in New York. He had a good job, a wife, three sons, and some savings. Then he started soaring in earnest, logging more hours in a year than all the rest of the club members combined. He took the club glider to Cooperstown, where he found a tow pilot who would pull him aloft winter and summer. Within a year, he had bought his own glider, a Blanik (a sturdy medium-performance metal ship made in what was then Czechoslovakia). It was in just such a plane that he had had his only aerotow in Hungary. He sold the Blanik two years later before moving to Arizona.

Les has a certain style, which endeared him to me and many others. He says that his experiences with the military in Hungary taught him how not to treat customers and how not to teach students. When I called him late in the day—it must have been at least 8:00 p.m.—after landing at an auxiliary Air Force base in Arizona, he acted as if it were the most routine call in the world; he didn't betray any of the anxiety that, by that time, he must have been feeling. ("Where is that guy? Why hasn't he called?") "So the Air Force wants me to pick you up before 8:00 in the morning," he said. "I'll be there at 7:30." At 7:25, after my surprisingly comfortable night in the small cockpit of the Grob 102 and after a breakfast of water and cheese crackers, I heard the buzz of an approaching Piper Pawnee. It touched down at 7:30. As we were connecting the tow rope from the Pawnee to the Grob, Les said, "I'm going to fly as fast as this bird will go with a glider in tow, so you better trim nose down. I'll be flying close to some mountain peaks. Don't be alarmed. That's the way I like to fly." It was a very agreeable flight back to Estrella.

As to how Les likes to fly, here's his description of a show he put on in his glider many times at annual air shows held in Mesa, Arizona: "After my aerobatic routine, I would be at a thousand feet approximately over the point where I wanted to touch down. I'd dive down steeply to pick up speed, pull up to a 45 degree up angle, do a half-roll, and then finish like a loop from the half-roll into a vertical attitude, and continue over the top until I'm pointed straight down at the ground. I'd pull out of the vertical dive, leveling a foot above the ground, touching down on the taxiway and rolling to where the people were standing, opening up the canopy as I came to a stop."

Was Les crazy? No. He pushed the envelope, as they say, but he wasn't crazy. Just very, very skilled. "You know," he told me, "I had thousands of hours in gliders by the time I did this routine, and I didn't start doing it near the ground. I started doing it at high altitude, perfecting it there."

*L*es is a fierce competitor. Back in 1978 or 1979 he finished first in international competition in flying for speed over prescribed courses, and he has finished in the top five a number of times. He has also won aerobatic championships, and some of his students and protegés have done so, too. Once, for reasons that seemed to hinge more on personalities than skills, Les was excluded from being part of the American team in an international competition in Texas. He contacted a Hungarian pilot who was planning to come and compete, and that pilot, without ado, arranged for Les to get a Hungarian passport ("almost overnight," Les said), so Les traveled from Arizona to Texas to compete as a Hungarian. He finished a creditable 12th in a large field, and was not entirely disappointed to see a rival on the American team finish 18th.

I once asked Les if he had ever had any outlandings that led to interesting stories. And whether he had ever had an accident. "Well, a couple of outlandings that might qualify," he said, "and one accident for sure."

One outlanding came in Ohio during a contest in 1986. To get back to base, Les and the other pilots had to penetrate a nasty squall line containing heavy rain and strong downdrafts. I'll let Les tell the story: "There were screams on the radio. One guy went in there and got totally disoriented, with his speed building. He was screaming his head off. [He got control and survived.] I found a little area that looked just a little less grim than the rest. I was 6,000 feet above the ground when I entered the squall line and I was probably 200 feet above the ground when I came out. I can't see forward because the cold rain caused moisture to condense on the inside of the canopy. I can still see out the side, and here's this fenced yard, a big yard, and I'm in a 35 [a Schweizer 1-35, furnished to Les by the Schweizer factory in Elmira, New York], which is a very good short distance lander, really excellent. So I'm making the turn, and I see kids running out of the building—it was the backyard of a school.

"I said, 'Damn. I can't do this. I'm just gonna turn.' I can't see forward, I don't know what's there. So I put my glider into a side-slip so that I can go between two poles at the far side of the schoolyard and get the hell out of there. The moment I got through that opening, I kicked the rudder to straighten it, and I was touching down.

"It seems like only moments later this big guy is coming at me. I barely got out of the glider and he's just nonstop shouting. He's very angry and he's ready to punch me in the nose. He was telling me that I'm gonna drive my goddamn car with the goddamn trailer into his field and I'm gonna crush all his crops (he must have had a bad experience), and I'm saying, 'No, I'm not. No, I'm not. No, I'm not.' Finally, one of those 'No, I'm not's' stopped him. 'You're not? You're not gonna?' 'No,' I said, 'I'm not. So far I haven't done any damage to your crop. Here's my wheel; it's in a row between the crops. And my wing just went down after I stopped. I haven't damaged anything. My crew's gonna walk in. Piece by piece, we take the glider out of here to solid ground, out of your crop, and we're gonna put it into its trailer over there.'

He's quiet for a moment and then suddenly he says, 'Well.' We were just good friends from then on."

The other outlanding Les told me about occurred in a backyard in California, with quite a different reception. He was flying with a friend in a two-place Janus glider in the open class Nationals (any glider of any kind eligible). The friend, who owned the glider, wanted to ride with Les to gain skill in competition flying. They had started from Estrella and, in five or six hours in the air, made it to El Mirage, California, the site of the contest, in a single leg. Such competitions have a series of tasks assigned, one each day, chosen to be challenging but not impossible for the given day's weather. But one day they ran out of lift and out of luck. As Les tells it: "There's this house and it looks like its backyard *might* be big enough to land in. All the other area was kind of rocky. I didn't want to break my friend's glider, so I said, 'Wes, when I tell you 'Now' you pull the chute.' [The Janus has a parachute that can be popped to slow it once it's on the ground.] As we're crossing the fence I tell him 'Pull' and he pulled it and we stopped next to a small house with a nice porch in the back, with a couple of guys sitting there drinking beer. There's a cooler next to them, not fifty feet from where we stopped. One of the guys gets up, reaches into the cooler, grabs two beers, and brings them to us, just as if it were a totally everyday experience. No expressions of amazement. No nothing. They were as cool as the beer." Les and his friend Wes relaxed for a few minutes before calling for a crew to come with a trailer to get them back to base. They finished ninth in that contest.

Les admits to a number of close calls, "because of my nature." But he had only one accident. It was very public, and, in his words, it gave him a "terrible red face." In 1989, as he recalls it, he had been hired by a filming crew to do aerobatics and a low pass over a lake near San Francisco. The aerobatics, filmed from a helicopter, went well for the first two days. On the morning of the third day, he was up before dawn to prepare for his assignment—to skim low over the surface of a lake just at sunrise. A landing field was less than two miles from the lake shore, so Les figured that if he had enough speed flying a few feet above the water, he could pull up, translating some of his extra kinetic energy into potential energy, and make it to the field.

Here's Les's description of how that morning unraveled. "I'm at like 700 feet with the sun on the horizon and the sun's rays reflecting off the bottoms of some cumulus clouds, and I see the lake under me and the crew with the camera set up. I'm diving at the lake, very steep dive, and I'm pulling out and I'm steadying myself about three feet above the water and doing like 110 knots plus, and then I suddenly realize two wild ducks in front of the camera are gonna be taking off because they're seeing me and I'll be at their altitude when I get there. And sure enough it's happening just the way I visualized it. So I'm pulling up to clear the ducks because I don't want to hit 'em. I'm doing 90 knots or a little over 90 knots at this moment. This is right in front of the camera. As soon as I sense I'm clear of the ducks I'm pointing the nose down to go back to the same altitude, but I screwed up. I was looking at the water, and I should have been looking at the horizon.

"Visualize, there is no wind. The lake is a mirror. These puffy clouds with their white bottoms reflecting are telling me there's fifty more feet I can go. Actually, there's maybe six inches between me and the water. When I glance up at the horizon and realize how low I am, I'm adding the back pressure to pull up so I don't hit the water. Too late. There's a phenomenon that when the air flow speeds up, the pressure decreases. That's what happened to me. The bottom of the glider is curved and I got so close, suction dragged the glider down and the nose just went underwater. It broke off the nose up to my knees. This ship didn't have foot straps on the rudder pedals the way some gliders do. If my feet had been strapped to the rudders, I probably would have lost both legs.

"I was scooping up the water. I was in a flying suit. The water just goes up into my pants, fills up my chest area. The glider's nose is gone and the canopy is busted off. One thing you learn as a pilot is never to stop flying as long as you've got anything to work with. I pulled back on the stick. The glider, or what's left of it, springs about 20, 25 feet in the air, with water streaming out of the cockpit. It's all on film. The fiberglass layers in narrow strips are peeling off from the beginning of the break, all still attached at the end of the fuselage near the rudder, like streamers following this glider. But with all the weight shifted to the rear, the glider's nose wants to keep swinging up. I'm pushing hard forward on the stick, but even so, the glider is angled up at about 45 degrees.

By the time it gives up and stops flying, I've reached the shore. The tail touches down within about ten feet of the shore, and then, not with a big bang or anything, the whole fuselage stops on the ground. I didn't slide 50 feet."

Les ended up with a small blue mark on the little finger of his left hand. The glider's fuselage was done for, but the wings were salvaged. Les didn't feel like flying any more that day.

-6-
All of a Piece

I didn't meet Bob Buck until 2006, while I was working on this book. By that time, I felt that I already knew him well. Through his writing, he had been a shadow teacher and mentor to me for a long time. I knew that in the 1930s he flew DC-2s and DC-3s all over the United States for TWA (then Transcontinental and Western Airlines). In those days, a flight from Newark to Los Angeles—which needed two crews to complete—was as likely as not to stop in Pittsburgh, Chicago, Kansas City, and Albuquerque (with some of its passengers sleeping, or trying to, in Pullman-style berths). That was an express flight. Flights with less distant final destinations stopped more often. In his autobiography,* Buck describes a regular flight he made from San Francisco, starting with a twelve-mile hop to

---

* *North Star Over My Shoulder: A Flying Life* (New York: Simon and Schuster, 2002).

Oakland, then continuing to Fresno, Las Vegas, and Boulder City, Nevada. In the 1970s he flew 747's from California to Hong Kong, still for TWA (by then Trans World Airlines), a trip of more than 14 hours with no stops. In his later years, he took up soaring, and—what was most important for me—showed himself to be a gifted writer. He wrote enlightening and entertaining articles for a little magazine called *Air Facts*, a magazine that I devoured every month. I called it the flying magazine for mature adults. He also wrote two classic books, mainly for fellow pilots, *The Art of Flying* and *Weather Flying*. Updated editions of both are still in print. Then, as I happily discovered recently, when he was in his 80s he wrote the memoir referenced above.

One thing that Bob Buck taught me is that flying is all of a piece. An Ercoupe, a Super Cub, a DC-3, an LS-4 glider, a 747: They're all the same in essence, and the art of flying one of them is the same as the art of flying another. That doesn't mean, of course, that a pilot can step from one of them into another and fly it safely—or even know where to look for a gauge or reach for a lever. It means that a pilot flying any one of them is handling the same set of controls (pedals and a stick or wheel to control rudder, ailerons, and elevator), is concerned with the same issues of attitude and altitude and airspeed, is coping with the same weather, is trying to pull off a smooth landing, and is gaining the same kind of satisfaction from a flight well executed.

From my friend Chris Doig in the glider club, I learned the same lesson. She flies big jets for UPS one day, an L-19 tow plane or a glider another day, her little Aeronca Champ or a Cirrus four-seater another day. All of a piece, she insists.

Yes, there are common elements in every flight, but no two flights are alike, even in the same airplane. And for a reason. The sky is never the same. Air, clouds, fog, rain, wind, sun, stars, and moon. The sky is all of that, plus lightning in the distance and St. Elmo's fire dancing two feet away on the airplane's windshield. The sky is in turn blue, gray, black, orange, red, white. It can be eerily still or churning and angry. On a crystal day in the west, the sky seems to know no limit, stretching from horizon to horizon and from earth to infinite space. On a murky day in the east, it barely spans a village and is confined above by a ceiling you think you could reach out and touch. Inside a cloud, it contracts into a cocoon only big enough to hold one airplane. On an overcast, moonless night, the sky takes its leave of you. There is no sky. There is only you and your cockpit and the glowing instruments, disembodied from the rest of the universe.

The sky has moods. On one day, it lets you through as if it cares not a whit that you have left earth to invade its realm. On another day you wonder if the sky has decided to have some fun at your expense, tossing you this way and that like a die in a crapshooter's hand. On still another day, the sky seems offended by your presence. It hammers you with hail, lifts you and drops you back down at rates you can't control, as if telling you that it wants you to be someplace else.

ccording to my log book, I have flown from Socorro, New Mexico to Santa Fe and back about 200 times, most often in my beloved Beechcraft Bonanza, but sometimes in a Piper, Cessna, Mooney, or Bellanca. Depending on wind and weather, it's about a forty-five-minute flight each way. I loved every flight. Every one was special. Let me describe one northbound and one southbound flight just to illustrate the range of possibilities on this "commuter run."

On a September morning, Joe Taber and I are at the Socorro airstrip before 8:00. We preflight the plane and get aboard; I check the engine and controls, and taxi to Runway 15 (numbered to indicate its 150-degree heading, southeasterly). There is no cloud in sight and no breath of wind. As the plane lifts from the runway, Joe hits his stopwatch. He keeps statistics. We climb as smoothly as an elevator in a luxury apartment building on Manhattan's upper east side. I lower the left wing, we turn over Interstate 25, and head north, the Rio Grande on our right, the town and M Mountain (we have to look up to see it) on our left. Soon we pass over the mesa at San Acacia, looking down on the visible outlines of a long-gone pueblo and kiva, still harboring, as we know, a rich collection of pot shards. By the time we reach the Socorro radio beacon twenty miles north of town, we are climbing through 8,500 feet. We turn slightly right, level off at 9,500 feet, and start listening to radio conversation at Albuquerque. Off our right wing is the hundred-square-mile Burris Ranch. Weldon Burris's house reputedly has twenty-four bedrooms and twenty-five bathrooms. I never counted. I know that his hangar can accommodate a small jet with room left over for a few planes of the kind I fly. Beneath us is a Southern Pacific freight train headed east toward a pass in the Manzano Mountains. I say to Joe, "I think that's an ammunition train." I pull the nose up, roll sharply, and dive straight toward the train, pretending to fire a machine gun. Joe is only amused, not alarmed. He's endured this sort of thing before. Then we regain our lost altitude and continue toward Tijeras Canyon, holding 165 knots.

Close on our left is Belen (buh-LINN), with its burgeoning housing development east of the river, then Isleta Pueblo, with its white mission adobe church clearly visible. We can't make out the outdoor ovens where Isleta's famous bread is made. Further left is Ladrone Peak, and in the distance Mount Taylor, sporting a fresh coat of white this morning. As we get close to Albuquerque and talk to the controllers, we fly over what I think of as "dream city." Roads are bulldozed to look like a small city, and the lots, owned by easterners wanting to possess their own piece of America, all stand empty. Soon we are over Sandia Lab's "power tower," a giant experiment in harnessing solar energy, and then a series of bunkers southeast of the city that I am sure contain nuclear weapons. Those bunkers make me uneasy. I think back to the time I was flying very low across Kansas—to avoid stronger headwinds higher up—and suddenly passed directly over a missile silo, looking so incongruous, yet so innocuous, next to a farm house, a pickup truck, and a line of drying laundry. I still remember my first reaction: looking up to see if a Soviet missile was on its way down.

This morning, with perfect weather, we choose to fly over the cement plant in Tijeras Canyon and up the "back side"—that is, the east side—of Sandia Mountain. Off to our left, at about our altitude, we can see the ski lifts, standing ready. At this point, Albuquerque controllers lose interest in me and I in them. As the right wing tip comes abreast of the highest peak of the Ortiz Mountains, I reduce power and we start down. I want to cross the Santa Fe radio beacon at 7,000 feet above sea level, 700 feet above the ground. We nail it. We glide past the State Penitentiary. Joe can enjoy the view of the Sangre de Cristo range to his right and the Jemez Mountains ahead. I have to concentrate on air traffic and a smooth landing. We are cleared "straight in" to Runway 33 (heading 330 degrees, northwesterly). As the wheels touch the runway, Joe announces, "Forty-four minutes." We taxi to our usual parking spot, climb out of the plane and into a waiting Avis car, and head for the Statehouse via McDonald's.

It's 9:00 p.m. in the evening of a mean March day as I check out my airplane on the tarmac in Santa Fe, waiting for my three passengers to join me. We've been kept late by an interminable Senate hearing. It's that time of year when a late blizzard or an early thunderstorm can show up unannounced. Today, no blizzard, just snow flurries all day that kept me wondering whether I'd be in my airplane or in a Santa Fe hotel tonight. It's OK. An accumulation of less than two inches. And no thunderstorm, just roiling low clouds and strong west winds. It's "instrument weather"—that is, below the minimum ceiling and visibility needed to fly visually. We are going to be in for a bumpy ride through the clouds, but according to the forecast, we should be able to land at Socorro. In case the forecast is wrong, we have selected the airport at Truth or Consequences (sixty miles farther south), with a more favorable forecast, as our alternate.

I ask my passengers to make sure their seat belts are tight as we wait at the end of Runway 33 for takeoff clearance. The jouncing starts the moment we break ground. Briefly the runway lights rush by underneath. Then total blackness. Not because we have entered a cloud, but because northwest of the airport there are no lights, no cars, no houses. Low hills block our view of Los Alamos, hills that we must surmount but can't see. This is called the transition from visual flight to instrument flight, and it's sudden. My world becomes the cockpit. Albuquerque Center clears me to turn left and climb to 10,000 feet. I listen to airline captains reporting "chop" (turbulence) and inquiring whether there are any altitudes more benign than the ones they're at. As I get handed off to Albuquerque Approach Control, I know that I am following the Rio Grande Valley south, that Cochiti and Santo Domingo Pueblos will soon be sliding invisibly under my right wing. We are kept comfortably away from Sandia Mountain.

No sooner do I settle down at 10,000 feet than Approach Control tells me to go to 12,000 feet. That way they can route departing and arriving commercial planes beneath me. For this time of day, there are a surprising number of planes in the air, and there's a surprising amount of radio chatter. As I pass the Albuquerque radio beacon, Albuquerque's weather goes to pot. Commercial planes are being asked to hold or are being re-routed. Some private planes are trying to land and making "missed approaches." We have no information on Socorro. We just have to go and have a look. Approach Control sends me down to 9,000 feet and clears me for the instrument approach to Socorro. (I take pleasure in knowing that it was my initiative that led to the Federal Aviation Administration's approval of the approach a couple of years earlier.) Because of M Mountain, we are required to break off the approach if we don't see the ground when we are within 1,500 feet of it.

We start down at the Socorro radio beacon. My passengers seem to be taking all the jouncing in stride. But I'm sure they are as relieved as I am when we see lights— from cars on Interstate 25 and from houses in the village of Escondida—just as we reach the critical altitude. As suddenly as my realm had contracted to the confines of the cockpit as we left Santa Fe, it now expands to take in a big chunk of the sky and land. There is the college campus, there the warning light atop the mountain, and there the rotating beacon at the airport. I ease the plane lower and enter the landing pattern. The runway lights have been left on for me. I tell the controller in Albuquerque that my landing is assured and that I am canceling my flight plan. I do this in the air because we might lose radio contact once I am on the ground.

The pilot of a private plane who has tried twice without success to land at Albuquerque and is now in a holding pattern hears my call and asks to divert to Socorro. His request is approved. We hardly have my plane tied down and the luggage unloaded when we see and hear him approaching. My passengers, who have their own car, head on into town. I wait to help this stranger. With my guidance, he taxis his sleek twin-engine Beechcraft to an unoccupied tiedown space, and shuts down his engines. He is alone. He climbs out and extends a hand. "Thanks," he says. "I'm Michael O'Rourke, cardiac surgeon" (I'm using a fictitious name here). I resist the urge to say, "Hi, I'm Ken Ford, nuclear physicist." But he is a nice enough fellow. I take him to my house, where my wife Joanne is still up. Over some light refreshment we unwind, talking about the evening's weather and about flying, topics no pilot tires of. (He also tells me of a Socorro patient who came by to thank him for a successful operation. Dr. O'Rourke admitted—to me—that he accepted the thanks politely, although the only time he had ever seen the patient before was when he was stretched out unconscious on the operating table with his face obscured by a mask. The assembly-line methods seemed to produce enough income for a very nice airplane—and, for all I know, provided superior medical care, too.) I deliver the doctor to a local motel. In the morning, he flies uneventfully to Albuquerque and I go to my office, energized.

$\mathcal{T}$ here are two things the sky can do to you that pilots really don't like. One is to put a thunderstorm in your path. The other is to deposit ice on the wings.

Ice not only adds weight, it alters the air flow over the wing and can reduce lift. Up until the jet age it was a problem for airliners as well as private planes. The prescription when you encounter icing is simple: Do *something*. Descend to warmer air if that's possible. If not, climb, either to colder air (where, interestingly, icing is likely to be less severe) or to get above the clouds. (If you are among the fortunate few whose planes are equipped with de-icing equipment, you certainly activate that equipment, but may need to climb or descend as well.)

I recall a relatively short flight on a winter day from Albuquerque, in the center of New Mexico, to Hobbs, in the southeast corner of the state. Owen Lopez, a friend and a member of my Board of Regents, was on board the Mooney. We entered clouds soon after takeoff and were routed due east above the pass separating the Sandia and Manzano Mountains. Climbing through 9,000 feet, my vigilant passenger noticed the white coating on the leading edges of the wings at about the same time I did. "Don't worry," I said, "We'll just climb higher and get on top."

The controller readily agreed to my request for 11,000. At that altitude the clouds were still thick, and the ice was still building. I asked for 13,000 and got it. It took a while to get there. Because of the ice and the diminished performance of the engine at high altitude, the Mooney was struggling to get higher. Finally reaching 13,000, we found . . . clouds and ice. It seemed that the ice was hanging on but not getting thicker, an encouraging sign. But I still wanted to get out of the clouds. With the controller's acquiescence, we tried to go higher and finally found ourselves in beautiful clear air with bright sunshine at 15,000 feet. I wanted to hug the Mooney and I think Owen wanted to hug me. Since we had no oxygen on board, we didn't want to stay long at that altitude. (In fact, we were violating a Federal Air Regulation by being there at all. Above 14,000 feet, the use of oxygen is required. Most pilots, it must be admitted, regard this rule more as a suggestion than as law. Since I was adapted to living at 5,000 feet, I felt free to edge that altitude upward for a limited time when I had a good reason to do so. Still, it was a rule I paid attention to. The airplanes I flew had no oxygen, and in cross-country flying I never cruised above 13,000 feet.)

The ever cooperative controllers authorized descent at our discretion, and we made our way downward as the tops of the clouds got lower. When we let down through the remaining clouds and landed in Hobbs, there was still a telltale trace of white decorating the front of the wings. Owen tells me that he hasn't forgotten that flight.

I have shown too clearly in these pages my preference for western flying. In truth, every part of the country offers good reason to fly and no end of satisfaction in doing so. But I do have to say that it's easier to stay out of thunderstorms in the west, where they are normally separated by great swaths of clear air and can be avoided by going around them or turning back. (All to the good, since they may be even more murderous than their eastern brethren if you were to wander into one.) Actually, to give the east its due, one of the most beautiful thunderstorms I have ever seen was in Florida. It was late afternoon, I was about five miles to one side of a giant cylinder of what looked like cotton candy, tinged pink by the setting sun, and illuminated from within by the nonstop fireworks of lightning strokes—silent strokes, from where I was. The air I was flying through was as smooth and clear as at dawn. The cotton-candy column extended tens of thousands of feet above my altitude. With both its feet and its head touching gray flatiron clouds spread horizontally, the whole thing looked like a giant capital I in an illuminated manuscript.

Over Boston one summer afternoon I ended up inside what is known as an embedded thunderstorm—one that can take you by surprise because it is buried within other clouds.

I heeded the call of a school in the town where we lived that was raising money through a silent auction. My donation was a trip by air to Provincetown at the end of Cape Cod, with an afternoon at the beach. The winning bid was made by the Ditmores, a young couple with two small children. We met at Hanscom Field in Bedford around noon, and all climbed aboard the Bonanza. It was a lovely flight across the water, flown high enough to be within gliding range of land nearly all the way. Provincetown has one of those rare airstrips that is within walking distance of a beach.

After the Ditmores had their outing, we re-boarded the Bonanza in weather that was now turning murky and muggy. I took off visually and, once in the air, filed a flight plan for Bedford. Soon we were inside clouds. Then, right over Boston, whack! I hit a bump and my altimeter started winding upward. I throttled all the way back to idle and was still going up. Then came the downdraft. Even full power couldn't stop my descent at the originally assigned altitude. I called the controller and said, in my calm airline-captain voice, "Unable to maintain altitude."

The controller responded cheerfully, "That's all right. Everyone in your area is going up and down with you. Let me know when you get your altitude stabilized." Of course, he could see on radar that no one else was close to me, so he could afford to be jaunty. Just as we were in fact getting back to our assigned altitude, we broke suddenly out of the side of the thunderstorm into clear air with Bedford airport in sight.

As we taxied to parking, I said to my passengers, "I hope you didn't mind the rough air."

"Not at all," said Mrs. Ditmore, while her husband smiled. "It was fun. Thanks so much for a great afternoon." The children seemed happy, too.

As I had learned earlier, this was this couple's first flight in a small plane. I suppose they concluded that it was typical.

$\mathscr{P}rofile$

Chris Doig

Photo courtesy of Chris Doig

*I*n 2003, approaching her fortieth birthday, Chris Doig bought a house. It had four bedrooms, two-and-a-half baths, a one-car garage, and a two-plane hangar (if the planes are small). She keeps her Aeronca Champ there, and can provide indoor parking if a friend arrives by air. Her driveway, doubling as a taxiway, connects to a paved airstrip that she shares with half a dozen other fliers similarly connected. "This place is wonderful," she told me. "I've been so happy here. Sometimes I just have to pinch myself. I can't tell you. The first time I landed my airplane and pulled it up into the driveway, it was like the best feeling in the world."

An echo, perhaps of the time nearly thirty years earlier when, as a ten-year-old, she pedaled her unicycle triumphantly into the family's driveway (while dribbling a basketball). She was quite a kid: master of the extra-tall

125

"giraffe" unicycle, one of only three girls on the local Little League team, and a member of a Little League all-star team. The skills of those days hardly relate to the skills needed to fly airplanes, but they show a certain grit. Chris has mastered a lot of airplanes since then, and has kept them all right-side-up—except for the occasional deliberate roll.

When she's not flying her restored 1959 Champ, or cruising in a small Cirrus belonging to a flying club, or towing gliders in an Army surplus L-19, or piloting a glider herself, she is likely to be occupying the left seat of a wide-body Airbus A300-600 hauling 80,000 to 120,000 pounds of UPS freight, usually to or from Louisville, Kentucky, the main UPS hub—and usually at night. Her Airbus has something in common with her Champ and the Cirrus and the L-19 and the Grob 103 glider that she loves to fly: It usually carries two people. The other person on board the Airbus is her co-pilot, more properly called a first officer. Of course the Airbus A300-600 is capable of carrying more than two people, typically 300 or so when used as a passenger plane.

Chris's house is in a semi-rural part of Bucks County, Pennsylvania. Her soaring club, PGC (Philadelphia Glider Council), owns a small grass-strip airport in the same county, and her flying club, 907 Flight Squadron, flies out of the Doylestown Airport, also in Bucks County. But to get to her UPS job, Chris has to travel a bit farther. She drives to Philadelphia's main airport and flies commercially (or hitches a ride on a UPS plane if one is available) to wherever she is needed. Now that she has a certain seniority, she can opt for cities not too distant, such as Detroit or Chicago or Minneapolis—or sometimes Louisville, her official crew base, which can be a starting and ending point as well as a turn-around point. Back in her Douglas DC-8 days, when she had less seniority, she found herself flying to Alaska and Japan. When she moved on to Boeing 757s and 767s, with a bit more seniority, she flew mainly within the United States, but often to the west coast.

Here's Chris's description of a typical week: "Monday morning I commercial to whatever city. Last week it was Detroit. I drive down to Philadelphia. I get on US Airways and I ride to Detroit. Then I go to the hotel and crew rest until 9:00 at night. I get on the van. I go to the airport and I fly the plane from Detroit to Louisville. Then I sit for three or four hours while they sort and load all the planes (maybe 120 of them on a typical night). Then I fly the plane from Louisville back to Detroit. I finish at 6:00 in the morning. I go back to the hotel and I crew rest. Then the same all week long up until Saturday, when I get back to Detroit (or wherever I was flying out of). Then I can rest if I want to. Sometimes I opt not to and I get right on a commercial flight to go back to Philadelphia and then drive home."

C hris was born in 1963 in Plainview, NY, on Long Island, some thirty miles east of Manhattan. She's the third of four children, and the only pilot among them. Her father taught social studies in high school. Her mother was a social worker. It was her father who proclaimed to all his children, "Do what you love to do. It's the only thing that makes life worth living." And all of them did. Her older brother, David, loves music and runs a music school. Her older sister, Lisa, loves a challenge and found it in nursing. Her younger brother, Robert, wanted most of all to devote himself to a family, and he does (while working for a plumbing supply company).

According to sister Lisa, Chris was "the sweetest, nicest, most generous person, even as a child," although—out of character—she once got into a long fist fight with another girl who was a school bully. With people, Chris was somewhat shy; on the playing field, she was a dynamo.

When she was about fifteen, Chris got it in her head that she wanted to go hang-gliding. Her father, instead of discouraging her, said "I don't know anybody that flies hang gliders but I have a friend who flies sailplanes." He arranged for her to take a glider ride with his friend Dave Parker. In Chris's words: "That was it. I was hooked! Up until that point, I was pretty mediocre in school. I did participate in after-school activities—I was involved in soccer and softball, but I didn't really have much direction as far as what I wanted to do career-wise. But once I had that glider ride, the doors opened, the clouds parted, and I knew that's what I wanted to do."

Chris's father was, in her words, a "very smart man." When she started the eleventh grade in Hicksville High School, he made a deal with her. "If you buckle down, bring your grades up, and pass the Regents exams," he said, "and if you get a job to earn some of the needed money yourself, I'll approve your taking flying lessons and I'll contribute to the cost." That was all the incentive Chris needed. She kept her part of the bargain, and so did he. By the time she was sixteen, she was soloing two-seater and four-seater airplanes out of Republic Field in Farmingdale. She flew before she had a driver's license and often bicycled to the field. Because flying was expensive, she had to pace herself and she kept getting shifted from one instructor to another, so she was eighteen and in college by the time she earned her private pilot's certificate. Soon after that, still eighteen, she earned her glider pilot's license.

The idea of earning money as a pilot entered Chris's head at once, but, as she told me, "I never realized I was going to take it to the level I did. I never said 'I'm going to be an airline pilot.' I just wanted to fly and I thought wow, if I can get paid for it, it's going to be a great thing. But not for one second did I think, someday I'm going to fly a jet." As Chris knew or suspected, women were scarce in the ranks of professional pilots. Yet, armed by the will and the optimism acquired from her father, she plowed ahead.

Chris's parents—especially her father—wanted her to pursue a liberal arts education. She had other ideas, and when her parents saw the light in her eye, they backed her choice of the College of Aeronautics on Long Island. "If it wasn't an airplane, I didn't want to know about it," said Chris about higher education. Although flying planes was her real ambition, she decided to prepare for a backup career as an airplane mechanic. Part of the reason for this was her fear that she might inherit her mother's diabetes (she didn't) and be barred from flying. So after a two-and-a-half year program, she graduated with a license to repair airplanes and engines, and went to work in the shop of an FBO (fixed base operator) at MacArthur Field in Islip, Long Island. While there, she flew whatever she could whenever she could.

Like many a twenty-one-year-old living with parents, Chris chafed to get away and be on her own. Through her college's placement office, she found a job at Kaman Helicopter in Moosup, Connecticut, and moved there to do sheet-metal work on an assembly line. She continued to fly small planes at every opportunity, hopping to Martha's Vineyard and Nantucket and sometimes joining her new buddies (all male) in the Civil Air Patrol to fly practice missions or just head out for a Sunday morning brunch at some small air field.

Some pilots are loners. Charles Lindbergh comes to mind. Some are far more extroverted. In every flying club and at every small airport, you can find people whose first love is to sit around talking about flying (hangar flying, it's called), or just talking about anything to be sociable—to be part of the flying scene. Chris is a perfect blend of both types. She loves to sit at the controls of her Airbus at 35,000 feet, alone with her charts and her instruments and the stars (and, of course, the co-pilot next to her), making 300,000 pounds of airplane do her bidding. She also loves to hang around a small grass field, chatting with members of her soaring club even on a day when she's not flying a glider or a tow plane. That balanced approach to aviation started when she was a teenager, and still keeps her bubbling with enthusiasm about the joys of every kind of flying.

Many a young person—especially a young woman—finds the easiest way to deal with a romance gone sour is to leave town. That's what happened to Chris after a year-and-a-half at Kaman. She exited to North Carolina and moved in again with her parents, who, in the meantime, had retired to Belhaven in that state. She was 22, and now had in her pocket an instrument rating (authorizing her to fly in foul weather*), which she had acquired in an intense three-week flying-school program back on Long Island during a vacation from Kaman. Once in North Carolina, she earned a commercial license (authorizing her to be paid for flying), also in short order.

Before long, Chris had landed a job in the parts department of an airplane repair shop in Raleigh, North Carolina. Here the management, knowing of her commercial license and her zeal to fly, tapped her now and then to ferry a plane from one place to another. She wasn't exactly paid to fly, but it was on company time, so at least it was free. Then the social side of her nature kicked in, along with her wish to make a living flying, and she decided to become a flight instructor. Many an aspiring pilot starts in this way. It's the entry-level job in aviation. The instructor builds time in his or her logbook—the coin of the realm for getting an airline or corporate job—and gets paid for doing it.

For some, the instructor route to bigger things is a chore. Not for Chris. "I absolutely loved it," she told

---

* As noted in Chapter 4, pilots must also fly IFR (under instrument flight rules) whenever above 18,000 feet. Airlines generally fly IFR regardless of the weather.

me. She gained her Instructor's license in June 1986, when she was still 22, and started instructing at once at a small field near Raleigh (Raleigh East, it was called). A year later, she had added some 850 hours of flight time to her log book, bringing her total to about 1,200 hours. She felt ready to be a pilot-for-hire.

Meteoric is the right word to describe Chris's career from that point on. She spent six months flying bank checks around the south (always at night), then about two years flying for American Eagle, a regional carrier, where she started as a co-pilot and ended as a captain. In October 1989, a day before her 26th birthday, she was hired by UPS. By the time she was 32, she was a captain flying Boeing 757s all over the country.

The planes in which Chris flew bank checks bore some resemblance to those of Captain Eddie Ricketyback in the old Li'l Abner comic strip. When it rained outside, it rained inside the cockpit of some of these planes, and some of them had such tired engines that she had to check their oil at every stop. Back and forth, back and forth, she flew Piper Lances and Apaches and Aztecs from Raleigh to Richmond to Raleigh to Charlotte to Raleigh. The Lance is a single-engine plane with retractable landing gear (a little more sophisticated than the planes in which she had been instructing). Somewhere along here Chris earned a multi-engine license, authorizing her to fly the twin-engine Apaches and Aztecs. Any of these

Pipers can carry 800 pounds or so besides the pilot. That's a lot of checks.

While flying bank checks, Chris met and started dating Robert Kruemmel, another pilot. In 1988, they both went to work for American Eagle, and later that year they were married. I asked Chris if she and her husband had ever shared a cockpit. "Yes," she said, "sometimes we did, first with him in the left seat and me in the right, later with the roles reversed, since captains occasionally flew as co-pilots. Actually, I always felt uneasy with both of us in the same cockpit. I didn't really like to do it, but it could work out on holidays. One Christmas we flew together because it was the only way we could spend the holiday together."

After a year of so of marriage, they bought a Mooney, a four-seater with retractable landing gear, and flew it on some vacation trips, including twice to the west coast. That provided another share-the-cockpit experience. Chris claims that she was fairly relaxed ("laid back," as she put it) when her husband was at the controls of an airplane, or even driving a car, but that he was more antsy when she was doing the flying or the driving. "It was hard to fly with a spouse," she told me. "Everybody has their own way of flying an airplane. Some people are better at keeping their mouths shut than others."

Like all new hires at UPS, Chris started as an engineer. At that time, many large planes, in both freight and passenger service—including the Douglas DC-8 to which Chris was assigned—had a crew of three: a captain, a first officer, and an engineer. The engineer controlled the fuel, monitored a raft of gauges, and had some flying skills that might have been tapped in an emergency. The DC-8 is a four-engine jet similar in appearance to the Boeing 707. Those two planes were the first generation of large jets; they transformed the airline industry. Later-generation jets, such as the Boeing 757 and 767 and Airbus A300-600 that Chris eventually flew, have only two engines and are flown with a crew of two. (The reduced crew size had nothing to do with the reduced number of engines. It was merely a recognition that with improved instruments and improved engine reliability, the engineer who had been needed on the big piston-engine planes such as the Lockheed Constellation and the Douglas DC-6 was no longer needed.)

When Chris was divorced in 1993, she moved in briefly with her parents in North Carolina. "I think you're allowed to move in twice with your parents," she joked. Looking around for a place to settle, she had two criteria. One was to be near a UPS crew base. The other was to be where there were good opportunities to fly gliders and light airplanes. The northeast, closer to where she grew up, was appealing. Philadelphia, although not a crew base at the time, was rumored to be in line to become one, and the Philadelphia area offered good opportunities for recreational flying. Chris chose Doylestown. UPS didn't object. At once she joined up with PGC, a soaring club, and before long the 907 Flight Squadron flying club.

I was a member of PGC at the time, flying gliders and tow planes. Chris stood out, of course, because she was young, good-looking, and then the club's only female tow pilot. She was also friendly. And, to me, awesome. Here was a seemingly ordinary person who actually flew monster jets and therefore lived, I was sure, on some higher plane of existence, from which she descended on weekends to consort with the likes of me.

Making her way in a male-dominated world, Chris had learned how to be "one of the guys." Chris is neither frilly-feminine nor tough tomboy, but some happy mean between the two. She has the charm and infectious laugh of a Carol Burnett. There is no missing her enthusiasm for flying and her affection for people. She can wax equally eloquent on the sensual pleasure of bringing the tow plane in for a good landing on grass or the transcendental pleasure of watching the northern lights from her Airbus cockpit at 3:00 in the morning.

After buying their Mooney, Chris and her husband decided it would be fun to keep it at home. They contracted to build a house on a private airstrip called "Eagle's Landing" in Pittsboro, North Carolina. As it turned out, Chris enjoyed that lifestyle for only two months before her divorce, but the concept stuck with her and lost none of its appeal. Ten years later, thanks to a secure job and the escalated value of her Doylestown town house, she was able to think seriously about just such a move. She found the perfect place close at hand, bought it, and in 2003 taxied her Aeronca Champ up her new driveway on Elephant Path.

Here's Lisa Conner on her younger sister: "As a child she was cute as could be with her Buster Brown hairdo. Now she's a terrific pilot. I have flown with her often, always with total confidence. I'd rather fly in her little plane than be a passenger on a commercial jet. We are all proud of her."

-7-

All Kinds of Air, All Kinds of Flying

My friend Ron Hamm likes to say that my picture is on a *Wanted* poster in the Brownsville, Texas Post Office. Ron was the Director of Public Information at New Mexico Tech. He accompanied me on a flight to Mexico City in my Bonanza in December 1981. Joe Taber, Director of Tech's petroleum research center was also along. We went as the guests of Gulf Oil's representative in Mexico City, intending to talk about possible joint research efforts with Gulf and the Mexican oil company Pemex. As it worked out, not much developed in the way of joint research, but it was worth a try, and it was a pleasant trip.

On the way down, I carefully followed the rules: stop in El Paso to check out with U.S. Customs; once airborne, talk to radar controllers before crossing the Rio Grande; land in Juarez to check in with Mexican Customs; proceed on course. Although it was a crystal-clear day, we flew under instrument control, providing the comfort of being in touch with ground controllers (a visual flight plan would have been sufficient to meet Mexican requirements). After a rest stop in Torreon, where our eyes popped at the number of impressive planes with Mexican license numbers parked on the ramp, we made our way on into Mexico City, whose high plateau was awash in smog, making the instrument control quite welcome.

Two days later we climbed into the Bonanza and called Mexico City ground control. In pretty good English, the controller said, "Bonanza 29 Sierra, you're number 52 for pushback." (Throughout the world, air traffic controllers speak English.) I found the term "pushback" only quaint, since I knew we would taxi forward, not be pushed backward like the big boys. But I was a little alarmed by the number 52. That sounded like a long wait. Then a few moments later, I heard the transmission, "Trans World 81, number 45, you're cleared to taxi." The wait wasn't so long after all.

We were on a triangle trip, headed this day for Houston, so the route was northeast from Mexico City. Once out of the smog, we punched through a few clouds, then had clear air again for our landing in Matamoros, the final stop in Mexico. After checking out with Mexican Customs, we clambered back into the plane and I hopped across the border to Brownsville to check in with U. S. Customs. Only I was forgetful. I didn't use my radio to call U.S. Radar before crossing the border, as I was supposed to do. In Brownsville, a Customs agent asked me why I hadn't contacted radar controllers before entering U.S. airspace. I had to say "I forgot." Looking dubious, he typed my aircraft number, N5929S, into his computer. In a few moments, a warning on the screen began to flash. My airplane was on their "wanted" list. It was suspected of having transported marijuana illegally across the border. Out came all our luggage. In came the sniffer dogs. The agents looked in every cranny of the airplane and had the dogs sniff even the propeller "spinner," an aluminum cone that sticks out from the hub of the prop.

Finally, they began to believe that we were not smugglers. Perhaps the integrity of my good Quaker friend Joe Taber was written all over his face.

"Where did you get this airplane?" one of them asked. I told them that a friend and I had bought it from Ray Smith. (Ray Smith, as I mentioned in Chapter 3, managed the Socorro airport and had "kept me flying"— first in his various planes, then in this lovely Bonanza that he sold to my friend Lynn Orr and me. I liked Ray because I like people with passion. His passion was flying. Despite different backgrounds and different educations, we operated with mutual respect. In our dealings, Ray was totally trustworthy and trusting. When, later, he did time in a Federal prison in Texas, I grieved, but didn't judge.)

"How long have you had it?" asked the agent. I told him. It wasn't long. Then they let us go. Later I had to wonder: Was I an unwitting contributor to Ray's brush with the law? I'll never know.

To round out a splendid day in the air, we flew low over the curving Gulf beaches of Texas most of the way to Houston. From down low, one can study the comings and goings of Earthlings below. It may also be the safest place to be—especially when Navy jets from the Corpus Christi Naval Air Station are screaming overhead.

Another place where down low is the safest place to be is the northern extension of the White Sands Missile Range in New Mexico. Most of the huge Range is off limits to private airplanes, but we were allowed to fly across its northern end if we kept below 1,000 feet above the ground. Above that, jets were roaring around in simulated combat or maybe just having fun. Using this pathway was a useful privilege, since otherwise an eastbound flight out of Socorro would have had to detour fifty miles or so out of the way. I liked nothing better than to depart Socorro on a clear, quiet morning headed for Roswell or Hobbs or maybe Houston, cross the Rio Grande, climb gently over some hills east of the river, then descend toward the desert floor of the missile range. Since the jets were not always scrupulous about keeping at least 1,000 feet between themselves and the ground, it made most sense to skim along 300 to 500 feet up, from where you could nearly see the jackrabbits and could at least imagine the rattlers. One pilot friend remarked to me as we flew low across the range, "If we were flying any lower, we would get a ticket for speeding."

Toward the eastern side of the range, it was necessary to climb to clear some low mountains, the ones that were lit up before dawn on July 16, 1945, when the first atomic bomb was detonated at the nearby Trinity test site. After topping those mountains, 1,000 feet or less above their trees, I'm through the range. Approaching Carrizozo, I can climb to cruising altitude, but I do so a little reluctantly.

One of the oldest and least apt sayings about flying is that it is hours of boredom punctuated by moments of stark terror. What could be further from the truth? As a pilot (or, for that matter, as a passenger with a friend at the controls), I have never been bored and never terrified. If there are any pilots who are bored or terrified in the air, they should really give up flying and look for other ways to spend their time.

The most eloquent writers on flying (Saint Exupery, for instance) have managed to convey something of the feeling of flight in small planes to those who have not experienced it directly. Lesser writers manage only to convince the reader that the experience is meaningful to the pilot. I can probably do no better. Sometimes it's exhilarating. Sometimes it is breathtakingly beautiful. Sometimes it is like feeling one's way through a miasma. Sometimes it is like riding a roller coaster. Sometimes it is like driving a four-wheeler through a rock quarry. To me "satisfying" is the one word that most nearly captures all of the experiences of flying. That sense of satisfaction, of everything working the way it should work, of the person and the environment being in harmony, goes with a dawn takeoff in silky smooth air and no breath of wind; with flight inside a cloud when every instrument is pegged just where it should be; with straight flight in a glider zipping under a cloud street without gain or loss of altitude; with a steeply banked turn over a pine forest below a snow-capped peak; with a long steady descent ending just where it should at pattern altitude; with the gentle thunk of a good landing (or, best of all, the sound of tires brushing blades of grass before the plane settles onto an unpaved surface).

Only once have I had the pleasure of piloting an open-cockpit plane. This was a home-built Starduster that Ray Smith acquired somewhere. Because it was categorized as "Experimental," he had to log ten hours in it without a passenger before he could take anyone up in it. He enlisted my help to build this time, and I was more than happy to oblige. I put on a helmet and goggles, and even added the flourish of a scarf. Ray explained the Starduster's idiosyncrasies, chief among which was its tendency to go in a direction of its own choosing just after landing (it was a tail dragger). So I took it up for a few flights near Socorro and around the college's own M Mountain, and, with agile footwork on the rudder pedals, managed to keep it on the runway after landing. Unfortunately, the builder had mounted a propeller on it that was either too large or had blades with too large a pitch (that is, took too big a bite out of the air). The engine wouldn't rev up to its full rated speed, making the Starduster a very anemic climber, hardly what one expects from an open-cockpit biplane with a helmeted and scarved pilot. I think Ray decided it wasn't the best plane to keep around for offering rides to the public. He found a buyer and the Starduster soon disappeared from the airport.

*M*y advice to pilots who love tail draggers but can't lay hands on an open-cockpit plane is: Tow gliders. It's the next best thing. In hot weather, most tow planes can be flown with at least one window open. Even with the windows closed, they can be drafty enough to provide at least a little wind in the face. The interior of a tow plane is, as likely as not, Spartan, with cables and wires exposed to view. Typically, a tow plane is a stick-and-rudder tail dragger. I'm not sure if any airplane has ever been designed specifically to tow gliders. Every tow plane I have seen was designed for another purpose and adapted for towing. One of the most popular in America is the Piper Pawnee, a single seater designed to be an agricultural spray plane. Its designer, the same Fred Weick who was responsible for the Ercoupe, put great emphasis on safety. He wanted ag pilots who abruptly encountered a tree, a fence, or a plowed field to walk away from the experience. The pilot sits high. Between him* and the engine is a 200-gallon tank to hold pesticide (empty when towing!). Around him is a scaffolding of steel tubes.

Another popular tow plane is the Piper Super Cub, noted for its rugged simplicity and its ability to get in and out of small fields. Since the Super Cub has two seats (one behind the other), it can be used to train tow pilots. It's not something that can be done well without instruction and practice. My favorite tow plane is the L-19, also known as the Cessna 305A, and also known, in the Army, as the Bird Dog. My soaring club near

---

* There may be some women flying spray planes, but I've never heard of one nor met one.

Philadelphia owned two L-19's, both of them veterans of Vietnam, I believe. The Army used the L-19 (its Bird Dog) as a low-level observation plane. Like the Super Cub, it has tandem seating, a high wing, and a tail wheel, and can get in and out of small, rough fields. Unlike the Super Cub, it is all metal (the Super Cub being mostly fabric covered). It can fly as slowly as 60 miles per hour or as fast as 120 (flat out). With its enormous flaps deployed, it can descend at a steep angle for landing.

A typical tow goes like this. The tow pilot, dragging a thin 200-foot nylon or polypropylene rope,* taxis into position 50 to 100 feet ahead of the glider that is awaiting takeoff. The glider, with pilot aboard, sits with its wings canted so that one of them rests on the ground. An assistant on duty connects the free end of the line to a special hook located under the forward part of the glider—or, for some gliders, right at its front end. When the glider pilot signals that he or she is ready for take-off, this assistant—usually a fellow pilot, sometimes an eager teenager aspiring to be a pilot—walks to the end of the left wing and holds it off the ground so that the wings are level, then waves a small flag back and forth in an arc between about the 4 o'clock and 8 o'clock positions. The tow pilot, seeing this signal in a rear-view mirror, "takes up slack," taxiing cautiously ahead until a slight tug tells him or her that the rope is taut. The

---

* At one end of the rope there is usually a "weak link," designed to snap under a sudden load that, by regulation, must be at least 80 percent of the glider's maximum weight (loaded) and not more than twice the glider's maximum weight. It will hold fast under normal towing conditions, but can give way if an emergency creates a sudden large tension in the rope.

assistant at the end of the wing then swings the flag through a full circular arc and the tow pilot applies power. (This isn't the only technique that is used. Sometimes the glider pilot gives his signal of readiness by waggling his rudder; sometimes the tow pilot and the glider pilot communicate by radio.)

Unless there is a brisk headwind, the glider pilot can't keep the glider wings level during the very first part of the takeoff run. The assistant at the end of the left wing must be a wing runner, first striding, then dashing forward while holding the wing, trying not to be a "human aileron"—that is, trying to avoid pushing the wing upward or downward. The glider pilot quite quickly gains aileron control and the wing runner (who couldn't keep up for long anyway) steps aside.

Accelerating down the runway, the glider pilot uses the ailerons to keep the glider's wings level, the rudder to keep the glider lined up behind the tow plane, and the elevator to hold the nose at the right attitude, then to lift the glider from the runway. A few hundred feet down the runway, the glider will be in the air, but the tow plane not yet. Once the tow pilot leaves the ground and starts to climb, both the glider pilot and the tow pilot have a few minutes of concentrated effort ahead of them. To begin with, they must be alert to the possibility of a rope break. If this occurs before an altitude of about 200 feet is reached—which has been known to happen—the glider pilot isn't high enough to safely turn back to the field and must look ahead for a place to land. At most fields where gliders are towed, there are designated places for such emergency landings. As in all aspects of flying, avoiding surprise is the biggest contributor to safety. Instructors like to do simulated rope breaks by disconnecting the glider from the tow rope without warning, but they never do this below an altitude where turning back to the airport is a possibility.

The glider pilot's task during a tow is to keep the glider centered behind the tow plane, moving the glider gently left-right and up-down as needed. In turbulent air, this can be a struggle, as the air constantly juggles the relative position of the two aircraft. When the glider gets out of position, the glider pilot tries to ease it back where it belongs without adding too much tension to the tow rope or letting the tow rope go slack or, if it does go a little slack, without jerking it as it straightens out. Among towing tales of horror that I have heard but thankfully never witnessed or experienced are a tow rope looping around a glider's wing, and a glider flaring suddenly so high just after takeoff that the tow plane is tilted nose-first back into the ground.

The tow pilot's goal is, above all, steadiness. He or she tries to maintain a fixed speed, keep the wings level during straight flight, and make turns at a reliably constant angle of bank. Depending on the glider pilot's experience and the day's level of turbulence, this may require dance steps on the rudder pedal and a quick hand on the stick. The speed to be nailed during the tow may be 70 or 75 or 80 miles per hour, depending on the particular glider being towed, and sometimes as little as 60 (for an antique open-cockpit clunker) or as much as 90 miles per hour (for the highest-performance fiberglass ship).

The decision to release from the tow is made by the glider pilot, who likes to find lift (with the tow pilot's help) before pulling the release handle. On a summer afternoon in New Mexico with thermals popping everywhere, this could be at 1,200 feet above the ground. On a marginal day in Pennsylvania with scattered, weak thermals, it could be at 4,000 feet. Searching for a wave, or planning an acrobatic flight, or with a paying passenger on board, the glider pilot might hang on even longer. The usual technique (not practiced everywhere) is to release from a taut rope so that the tow pilot is immediately aware of what has happened. The glider then banks to the right, the tow pilot—after checking in the rear view mirror that the glider is indeed free—to the left. (Who turns right and who turns left is merely a convention. What the two pilots want to do is get quickly well away from each other; the turns help.) When towing, I have sometimes had a glider release from a slack rope, leaving me uncertain whether the glider was still attached or not. One indicator that the glider is no longer there is a sudden increase in the rate of climb. Another is that I can't see the glider in the rear view mirror. Neither of these indicators is definitive, however. I might have entered a thermal, accounting for the increased rate of climb. The glider might have got so far off center as to disappear from view. So I have to continue climbing and looking for a minute or so until I can safely conclude that the glider is gone. Once sure that there is no glider in tow, I hasten down for the next tow, although not so speedily as to overcool the engine. With 200 feet of tow rope stretched out behind me, I must approach the runway high enough to avoid snagging a tree or a fence or a spectator's parked car.

The tow rope can, in fact, be released at either end. Only once in 1,635 tows have I, as a tow pilot, had to reach for the release handle. On that occasion, I was being yanked this way and that by the glider behind me, and the rope seemed to be going taut, then slack, then taut. When I couldn't see the glider in the rear view mirror, I decided that things were getting out of hand and I released the rope. As it turned out, the glider pilot reached the same conclusion at about the same time and also released the rope. So I landed back at the airfield, he landed back at the airfield, and the rope landed in a neighboring farm. Since we had a pretty good fix on where we were when the rope came unmoored at both ends, we were able to retrieve it later that day.

$\mathcal{P}rofile$

Ray Smith

The only time Ray Smith landed an airplane with its landing gear up, he managed to do only $2,000 worth of damage. He artfully put the Cessna 310 down so it skidded on its jackstands (heavy pads near the center of the plane that are used for jacking it up for maintenance). In the few seconds he had available between the time the gear warning horn sounded and the plane's belly mated with the Socorro, New Mexico paved runway, he cut off the fuel supply to the two engines and managed to get one propeller stopped in the horizontal position. The other one was turning slowly enough so that when it hit the pavement it wasn't much damaged.

What good is a gear warning horn if it sounds off too late to be of any use? Not much. The horn is activated only when the gear is up *and* the engine is running at very low power. (Otherwise the horn would be blaring away during normal flight.) Since Ray carried some power in the approach until he flared for landing—typical for this airplane—he got the warning too late to abort. He remembered, he said, what more than one old pilot had told him: "When this happens, land straight ahead, do the best you can with it. If you apply power and try to climb that thing, it's gonna go ahead and sink 'cause you've already got it behind the power curve and if it does, the props'll catch the pavement and rip the engines off and you'll cartwheel." Then Ray might have had to add a zero or two to the $2,000 number.

Since Ray could fix the plane himself, he figured he was better off not telling the insurance company about it, and he didn't. But an accident is an accident. He had to report it to the Federal Aviation Administration. He called an FAA fellow he knew in Albuquerque. Here's Ray's account of that conversation: "He said, 'What happened, Carl Ray?' 'Well,' I said, 'I forgot to put the gear down.' He said, 'You forgot?' I said, 'Yes, I forgot.' He said, 'I ain't never heard of anybody ever forgetting. It always malfunctions or something, but you actually forgot to put the gear down?' I said, 'I did.' 'Well,' he said, 'I don't even need to come down there. I think that's the first time anybody's ever told me the truth.'"

*L*ater on, some Federal agents did come to see Ray. They wanted him to tell their version of the truth. They believed that some Socorro County officials and at least one State Police officer were engaged in a lucrative form of drug business—catching drug smugglers as they drove north from El Paso or Las Cruces, helping themselves to the smugglers' drugs and money, and then sending the smugglers on their way (or back for more). According to the Feds, Ray Smith must have known what was up and could tell a grand jury all about it, since he had often flown these possibly unsavory characters around the state, perhaps sometimes when they were making deliveries. Like others in Socorro, Ray suspected but didn't know. He says he told the agents: "I make it my business not to know other folks' business. I can't go before the grand jury and help you out, because I'd have to lie, and I ain't going to do that, 'cause I really don't know what these folks are doing." According to Ray, one of the agents responded, "Well, the state attorney would tell you what to say." "That's the problem," Ray answered.

Then, as Ray tells the story, the agent played his ace. He said, "We've got an indictment on you out of Oklahoma." "I don't know what the problem is in Oklahoma, but I'm not going this route," Ray answered. Ray was stubborn. He didn't testify against his Socorro friends, and he wound up in a Federal prison. It seems that he had sold an airplane to a man in Oklahoma, an airplane that later crashed in Florida on its way back from South America with a load of drugs. The new owner had neglected to change the registration of the plane he bought, so when it crashed, the authorities called Ray Smith to tell him that his airplane lay in pieces in Florida. The question of ownership got straightened out, but the link to the drug smuggler didn't. To lighten his own sentence (as Ray tells it), the Oklahoma kingpin of the drug ring implicated ten other people as accomplices, including Ray—even though he was unable to point to Ray sitting in the courtroom, and even though there was no link other than the sale of the plane. Ray spent a little over a year in minimum-security prisons, one in Arizona, another in Texas.

I wrote a letter to Ray when he was in the Texas prison. I didn't get an answer. Later, by chance, I ran into him in Socorro, where my friend Lynn Orr and I had stopped for gas while flying across the country. While Lynn's plane was being gassed, I asked the airport manager if he had any information about Ray, who no longer lived there. "There he is," he responded, pointing to a Cessna 172 that was taxiing by. Sure enough. I flagged down the plane. We greeted each other warmly. I asked Ray if he had received my letter. "Yes, Ken, I got the letter," he said. "Thanks. But I just didn't know how to answer it."

Much later, when I sat down with Ray to review his life, he said to me, "Ken, I ain't never used drugs. I ain't never sold drugs. I ain't never flown drugs." I choose to believe him. He dealt squarely with me, and, from all the evidence, with the rest of the world.

ay Smith was born in Mountainair, New Mexico in 1935. His parents operated a farm in Gran Quivira, about twenty-five miles south of Mountainair. Ray's interest in aviation was first tweaked as a child when he looked up in the clear skies above his remote part of New Mexico and saw Air Force fighters firing away at gliders being towed behind transport planes. He sometimes found ammunition belts in his family's pastures. By the time he was fifteen, he was fascinated by airplanes and decided he had to have a ride in one. "I got me some money together," he told me, "and went up to Albuquerque and paid them to give me a ride. Their pilot took me up in a 1947 Beechcraft Bonanza V10. I was really blowed away by it."

After completing grade school in Gran Quivira, Ray went off to high school in Mountainair, but dropped out after two years to go to work. Maybe that airplane ride showed him the advantages of having a little money in his pocket. He moved to Socorro, some sixty-five miles from Mountainair, and did farm work for a couple of years, working alongside Mexican "wetbacks," as they were called in that part of the country. "Then," as Ray tells it, "I got a job with the Ford dealership there as a mechanic's helper and a parts chaser. That led to becoming a mechanic. Pretty soon I was pretty knowledgeable about vehicles." For the rest of his life, there wasn't much that Ray couldn't fix.

Ray itched to fly, but for some years he couldn't put together enough money to do it. Then, when he was about twenty-five, he moved north to Grants, New Mexico, where uranium mining was propelling a hot economy, and got a job with a truck shop. "Then," he said, "I went to making money. Well, it wasn't long 'til I had enough money saved up to buy a Taylorcraft." (The Taylorcraft is a fabric-covered two-place taildragger similar to an Aeronca Champ.) Ray went to Albuquerque, parted with his savings of $1,200, and found a fellow (who may or may not have had a pilot's license) willing to fly his new acquisition out to Grants for him. "He made it," said Ray. "Then I got me an instructor and went to work."

He soloed after five hours of dual instruction, then continued to learn by flying as often as he could. He hung out in all his off hours at the local fixed-based operation, volunteering to help with maintenance or whatever else needed doing. Pretty soon, the manager, "Swede" Axelson, was letting Ray fly an assortment of planes. As Ray tells it, "Right away, it seemed like I could fly anything." When a Cessna 195—a large plane, much more of a handful than the Taylorcraft—arrived at the field, Axelson asked Ray, "Can you fly it?" "Hell, yes," answered Ray. "It's got wings, don't it?"

Like a lot of good pilots who put on a show of reckless bravado, Ray was in fact meticulously careful (it didn't hurt that he was a superb natural pilot). Before taking off in the big Cessna, he read the manual, sat in the cockpit and studied all the knobs, handles, and gauges, and talked to pilots who were experienced in the plane. That was his technique for everything he flew after that. "Another thing I learned in the years I flew," Ray told me, "don't underestimate anyone. You can learn something almost from anybody. It may not be everything, but if you just listen to 'em, sooner or later they'll come up with some point that's of value to you."

Briefing him on the Cessna 195, one veteran pilot said, "Just watch it. When you get it on the ground, you're not through 'til you tie it down." "And he was right," said Ray. "It wasn't bad, but..." Every taildragger needs careful rudder-pedal footwork on the ground, and the Cessna 195 more than most.

Later, Ray bought a Cessna 195 for himself, getting it from an Albuquerque flying club for only $4,000. It turned out that the club was anxious to get rid of it because it was so difficult to handle on the ground that no club member wanted to fly it. The club's mechanic had mistakenly connected some cables so that when the rudder swung left, the tail wheel swung right. When Ray picked up his new plane and took off from a grass strip, he thought, "Boy, this thing's pretty wild." When he landed it on the paved runway at Grants, he concluded, "It really *is* wild." He inspected the tail cone, found the problem, and fixed it. Then he had some fun with the people who had sold him the plane, telling them how much he was enjoying the docile 195 they sold him.

*O*nce embarked on buying airplanes, there was no stopping Ray. At first he bought and sold planes just to enjoy variety in his flying. He made his money as a mechanic, not as a pilot or airplane entrepreneur— although occasionally he could turn a small profit when he sold a plane. Ray estimates that he has owned at least 150 airplanes, from the little open-cockpit Starduster biplane that I had a chance to fly to big twin-engine Beechcrafts and Aero Commanders capable of carrying a couple of thousand pounds. He was kind enough to let me fly quite a few of them.

During his time in Grants, Ray was married ("for a few years," he says). He also moved for a while to Gallup—about 60 miles farther west—and he hopped down to Socorro now and then. He figured that Socorro might be a good place to settle down and make use of both his skills: flying airplanes and fixing trucks. He thought the town was ripe for a truck shop, and he discovered that quite a few students at the local college, New Mexico Tech, were interested in learning to fly. To meet the first need, he opened a truck shop on the main highway. To meet the second need, he bought a Cessna 172 (very often used as a trainer), and started renting it to students. He wasn't a licensed instructor himself (although he had passed the instructor's written exam), but there was a lot he could teach students by flying with them, and he did. He brought in instructors from other towns to polish the skills of the student pilots, solo them when they were ready, and recommend them for licenses when they reached that point.

A couple of years after moving to Socorro, Ray was appointed manager of the local airport, and that's where I saw him often. His base salary from the city was $200 per month. Supplementing that meager base, he pieced together what he describes as a pretty good income. He made money from hangar rents and tie-down fees and netted about a dime per gallon of fuel sold. He rented planes, did charter flying, and bought and sold planes. Soon, he was in so much demand flying judges, county officials, professors, and ranchers around the state that he had no time to work on trucks, so he closed that shop. He married again and lived in a mobile home at the airport. I recall flying with him one night when we delivered John Slaughter, the director of the National Science Foundation, from Socorro to Alamogordo. On the way there, I sat in the right front seat, giving Dr. Slaughter the comfortable impression that he had a crew of two. On the way back, I sat in the left seat and logged a little twin-engine time.

What I knew about Ray when we both lived in Socorro was that he was a likeable guy, a trustworthy friend, and a gifted pilot. What I didn't know is that he loved not just airplanes, but heavy equipment, too. As it turned out, he was as much an artist with a giant bulldozer or excavator as with a Cessna 195. "An excavator—a big excavator—is my favorite piece of equipment," Ray told me later. "I can set in one of them and daydream and run it and just do anything with it. They're so versatile. You can do so much with one of 'em. You can dig a hole 20 feet deep and as big as you want it in just no time at all. You can cut a ditch four miles a day with one of 'em."

Along about 1981 or 1982, Ray was feeling burned out from flying day and night and doing everything else that managing the airport entailed. He went to Colorado to operate construction equipment. It was after a couple of years there that he ran afoul of the law and did time in prison. Once free, he moved to Alaska and found his niche there, where he could fly all kinds of planes in all kinds of weather into all kinds of landing strips, and operate all kinds of machinery—the bigger the better—on all kinds of terrain. Ray has logged somewhere over 13,000 hours in the air, from little two-seaters to Douglas DC-3s. He probably has about the same amount of time at the controls of bulldozers, tracked trucks, backhoes, front-end loaders, and excavators.

Ray's only airplane accident was the gear-up landing I described earlier. His only serious mishap in heavy machinery came when he was trying to get a big bulldozer across a creek that was stacked up with overflow ice, maybe forty feet of alternating layers of ice and flowing water. Three other Cats (Caterpillar tractors) got across, but his Cat, the heaviest of the lot, started listing and sinking. Miraculously, both Ray and the Cat survived. A tow cable helped his Cat get across. Ray, who emerged from full immersion, had to strip fast and dry out standing naked before a roaring fire in sub-zero weather. When I marveled at what he and his men went through—not just on this occasion, but generally in Alaska's back country in the winter—Ray said, " Those people I had working for me, they told me, 'We'd go for nothing on one of these jobs. You don't have to pay us. Just feed us.'"

I asked Ray if flying an airplane and operating an excavator had anything in common, and whether some heavy-equipment operators are naturals, just as some pilots are. First, he gave me his thoughts on natural pilots: "In my years of flying, Ken, I've taught a lot of people to fly. Some could fly an airplane but they weren't pilots. They lacked a little. You could do all you could do with 'em, but they still lacked a little bit. A natural pilot, he's different, but there's not many of 'em around. He's the guy that can handle about any situation and he's not stiff, he's limber. He'll just get in there and fly it 'til there's nothing left to work with."

In a piece of heavy equipment, Ray pointed out to me, you can't sit next to someone to teach them the way you can in airplane. "About all you can do with a piece of equipment is tell somebody about it and try to watch 'em work. There's generally not room in the cabs to get in with 'em, but you can maybe stand them up and do a few things and explain it to 'em and put 'em to work and watch 'em make mistakes. Pretty soon they're either an operator or not, like a pilot."

"You get a man," Ray went on, "in a little bit you can see he's either good or he'll just be—well, maybe he can run it, but you don't want to watch him if you can help it, you don't want to watch him very long, you want to go do something else."

I've never watched Ray run an excavator, but I'm pretty sure he's a natural. He can get as poetic talking about an excavator as about a Beechcraft or a Cessna. "Sometimes," he said, "a guy on the ground gets a misconception standin' there lookin' at somethin'. The guy'll tell me, 'You look like you're high on that corner.' I'd say, 'It may look that way, but it ain't.' He'd go get his transit and shoot it, 'I'll be damned,' he'd say. 'It's level.'"

Ray lives in Arizona now, where his principal vehicles are pretty mundane: a pickup and a Honda Gold

Wing motorcycle. But the last time I talked to him, he said that he does get on board a piece of heavy equipment now and then, and he's contemplating the purchase of yet another airplane—an ultralight in which he can putt-putt around the mountains and canyons near where he lives.

- 8 -

Buttoning Up and Getting Going

I was astonished the first time I saw a pilot drive up next to a parked airplane, jump from the car, jump into the airplane, and roar away. He wasn't being chased. He wasn't trying to evade the law. He wasn't trying to escape to another country. He was just being foolish. It's all too easy to get in a hurry, either in the air or on the ground, and do things that jeopardize safety. I have been guilty at least once of such transgression (which, red-faced, I'll describe below). Yet the professional pilots I have known, even the ones who like to project an image of swashbuckling, devil-may-care insouciance, always took care in the planning and execution of a flight. On the ground, they were prepared. In the air, they had a "way out." Even Charlie Boyd, swearing that if a Santa Fe Railroad train could get through Glorieta Pass on a stormy night, so could he, was being much less foolish than might appear. He knew the terrain intimately; he knew every quirk of his plane; he may even have known just where the railroad signal lights were located. Charlie died in bed at 78. Some pilots who are less skilled and less careful meet a more untimely end.

There are two parts to getting an airplane or glider ready for flight ("preflighting" it)—three parts, really, if you include getting the pilot ready. If the plane you are about to fly has an engine, you check the fuel supply, the gas caps, the oil, the visible hoses around the engine, and the pins or bolts holding the cowl in place. You examine the propeller for nicks and lightly touch the exhaust pipes to make sure they aren't loose. For either airplane or glider, you check that the hinges of the control surfaces (ailerons, rudder, and elevator) are in good shape, the tire or tires (the glider is likely to have only one) are inflated, and the hydraulic brake line is connected. Either standing next to the cockpit or sitting in it, you make sure that moving the controls has the desired effect on the control surfaces.

That's Part 1. Part 2 is making sure that you have on board what you need to have on board, divided into things you can reach in the air and things you don't need to reach until you have landed. Things that should be handy include whatever food and drink you may need en route, maps, a pen or pencil, a microphone, a headset with earphones if that's what you plan to use instead of listening to a speaker (the headset may have an attached mike), and, if you are flying on instruments, a knee pad to hold maps and to hold scratch paper for writing down instructions received from the ground.

If you have a passenger on board who hasn't demonstrated a strong stomach in previous flights, it's also highly advisable to have within reach a "Sic Sac®," a waxed paper container whose name tells you what it's for. (When I took my seventeen-year-old daughter Sarah up for her first glider ride—she had been flying with me in power planes since she was four months old—it was aromatically clear that a passenger on the previous flight had been ill without benefit of a Sic Sac. Poor Sarah, nervous anyway to be contemplating flight without an engine, began to feel queasy before we even got off the ground. Once we were airborne, she seemed OK, but as we spiraled up to 15,000 feet in a strong thermal, she asked, with a quavering voice, "Is this all you do, Daddy? Fly in circles?" Lift is not something a glider pilot likes to part with, but I did, and made Sarah's first glider flight a short one.)

Now, as to what you don't need to reach. Luggage, obviously, if you're going on a trip. It's a good idea to have emergency supplies somewhere in the plane, especially when flying in the West. When I lived in Socorro, I always carried in my baggage compartment a cardboard box containing a gallon of water, a flashlight, a blanket, and an extra sweater. If the engine quit in the middle of nowhere, I figured I would have a good chance of getting the plane down in a dead-stick landing without seriously injuring anyone on board. I felt much less sure that I would be found right away. Best to prepare for a night in the desert or maybe even a day or two. Indeed, as recounted in Chapter 4, I did once spend the night in a glider, although in that case I wasn't far from civilization. I stayed in the glider then just because I didn't want to leave it untended overnight, and so I would be ready for the early-morning tow.

Pilot readiness is more of an issue in a glider than in an airplane. If the pilot of a power plane feels the need for a bathroom stop or a snack or just the need to walk around and stretch, he or she can usually land before long to meet the need. In cross-country flying in an airplane, I usually tried for three-hour legs, and, for the first leg in the morning, I preferred two hours. The occasional four-hour leg felt long. If you are trying to get somewhere in a glider, flights are likely to be longer (unless, of course, you run out of lift and have to land where you hadn't intended to). My longest flight was seven-and-three-quarter hours (the one that ended at the abandoned Air Force base in Arizona). My diamond distance flight was seven-and-a-quarter hours. On such flights, stopping for a bathroom break or a snack or to stretch is not an option. The pilot has to be ready, and that means mentally as well as physically. Competition pilots have to be keyed up yet somehow calm. Some ridge flights in Pennsylvania and extending down into West Virginia or beyond have lasted as much as fourteen hours. On every glider flight aiming for distance, the pilot is busy every minute. That applies even to my modest efforts. As a result, the time passes quickly. I have found that when circling to gain altitude in a thermal and trying hard to get the most out of it—constantly adjusting the angle of bank, the speed, and the center of the circle—it's out of the question to even open a snack container or take a sip of water. The brief moments of refreshment have to wait for a segment of straight flight.

My silver badge required a flight of five hours. That was my first flight of such duration. I didn't have to go anywhere to meet that requirement. I just had to stay up. As I contemplated the task, I was more worried about my bladder than about staying aloft. As it worked out, I was in no great discomfort. I drank very little the morning of the flight, and made the requisite pit stop just before takeoff. I sipped a small amount of water during the flight (which took place in the hot, dry air near Moriarty, New Mexico). For long flights, different pilots have different strategies. Some just count on their constitutions to hold out as long as necessary. Some rig up some personal plumbing so that they can relieve themselves in flight as the need arises. Some wear adult diapers just in case. I practiced deliberate dehydration—in moderation. Many instructors and experienced glider pilots warn of the risks of dehydration, which are real, but keeping myself a little dried out seems to work for me. Half a cup of coffee in the morning, a few sips of orange juice, a couple of ounces of water before the flight, and a steady but limited infusion of water during the flight—perhaps only a half liter during the course of a long flight. I have suffered no ill effects of which I am aware. To be sure, come evening, a large root beer float and two cups of coffee seem in order.

𝒥 t's not easy to come clean about a serious goof-up related to preflight procedures, especially when, as in my case, it occurred after more than 1,700 hours of flight time. But here goes.

On a lovely late-December day in 1975, I took off from the Socorro airport in Ray Smith's Bonanza for a local sightseeing flight, with four of my children—then eleven, sixteen, seventeen, and eighteen—on board, and with the gust lock in place. If you're a pilot reading that sentence, you'll be horrified. If not, let me explain what a gust lock is and why taking off with it in place is a blunder of the first order.

When a small plane is parked, you don't want the ailerons and elevator snapping up and down in a gusty wind. So they are usually held in place, most often with something called a gust lock. It's a little bit analogous to the "Club," the anti-theft device that prevents the steering wheel of a parked car from turning. In the Bonanza, and in many other planes, the gust lock consists of a sturdy wire, a little thicker than clothes-hanger wire, inserted through a hole in the control column and through a pair of aligned holes in a surrounding cylinder near the instrument panel. With this wire in place, the column can't slide in or out (to move the elevator) and it can't turn (to move the ailerons). Taking off with the gust lock in place is definitely not a smart idea because the pilot then has practically no control over the plane.

There are two safeguards to prevent such an unfortunate event. First is a standard part of the preflight check, which is to move the control wheel in and out and turn it left and right to verify that the elevator and ailerons move freely under the pilot's control. Second is a red "flag." This is a small rectangle of metal, painted red, which sticks up in front of the instrument panel and blocks access to the ignition keyhole. The heavy wire of the gust lock makes a 90-degree bend, its horizontal part passing through the control column, its vertical part supporting the red flag. Even if the pilot neglects to check the freedom of motion of the control surfaces, the red flag is there to prevent the key from being inserted and turned to start the engine.

How did I evade both safeguards? I had flown the same plane earlier the same day and no one else had flown it in between. "It's already preflighted," I told myself. "Let's get the kids on board and go." But why didn't the red flag stop me? Because it wasn't there. It had been broken off a few weeks earlier, leaving the bend in the wire to serve as a handle. Ray Smith had brought it to my attention and warned me to be careful until he could get a proper replacement. I had flown the plane a dozen times with the broken gust lock.

Maybe I was talking to the children and thinking about them instead of the job at hand. For taxiing, the rudder pedals are sufficient. I lined up on the runway and started the takeoff run. Reaching takeoff speed, I pulled back on the wheel. It moved about a quarter of an inch. Unfortunately, that was just sufficient to launch the plane. I found myself flying about a foot above the runway, gaining speed but gaining no altitude. I knew instantly what the problem was. I reached for the gust lock and pulled. It didn't budge. It was held fast by the back pressure I was exerting on the control wheel.

One can do a lot of thinking in a few seconds. Something like the following was going through my mind. "If I ease the control wheel forward a bit to free up the gust lock, the plane will probably touch back on the runway, way too fast, and put undue stress on the nose wheel. The nose gear could crumple, the plane could even flip over. If I cut the power, same problem. The plane returns to earth too fast and with too much stress on the nose wheel. If I hang on, I might clear the fence at the end of the field and the terrain beyond, or I might not. I've GOT to get this gust lock out." I tried again, jiggling and then yanking the bent wire while still holding back pressure. It gave way. With bloody knuckles, I held up the gust lock for the children to see. Once we gained a little altitude, I told them what had happened. We continued our sightseeing flight.

It's easy to be judgmental about the man who jumped from his car into his plane and roared away, but I was—at least once—just as foolish.

$\mathcal{I}$ n instrument flight, the cockpit is an office. The pilot might as well be at a desk. Just like an office worker, he or she is receiving and processing information, communicating, doing a bit of paper work, and trying to control events without getting up. It's quite a different feeling when you're flying an airplane around on a lovely clear day far from any city or major airport, just to enjoy the scenery and experience the exhilaration of flight. Then, in the cockpit, you can imagine yourself in the driver's seat in a sporty convertible, having left the worries of the office behind. If you're lucky enough to be in an open-cockpit plane, it really is a convertible.

The cockpit of a single-seat glider is neither office nor sports car. It's a nest. The pilot roosts there. (Not since World War II have gliders accommodated a dozen or more passengers—and those gliders were designed only to head downward, not soar upward. Now single-seaters are most common. Two-seaters are needed, too, for training and for giving members of the general public a chance to fly without an engine. The occasional glider that holds three is still flying. I have never seen a four-seater.) The very existence of a cockpit in a glider is a concession to practicality. Ideally, for the most efficient flying, the body of a glider should be shaped like a pencil. But there is a limit to how slender the pencil can be. Within it must fit an oxygen bottle, an instrument panel, various handles and control cables, a retracted landing wheel, a barograph, at least a few supplies, and a pilot—up to a 200-pound six-footer in the LS-4. Let me describe the cockpit of that particular glider, the one in which I roosted on my successful diamond distance flight. It is typical.

The LS-4 cockpit is widest—about two-and-a-half feet—in the vicinity of the pilot's shoulders and elbows. Its height in the same area is about three-and-a-half feet. The pilot settles into a semi-recumbent position, with rump about one foot above the ground, eyes a little higher than knees, and legs extended under the instrument panel to rudder pedals located far forward where the glider's width is little more than one foot. Above and behind the seat is a helpful headrest; without it, the pilot would find it tiring to keep his or her head up, given the reclining angle of the body. Some would call the cockpit cramped. I call it compact. It does its job and it's actually rather comfortable.

On the summer morning of my diamond-distance flight, the thermals started popping in the late morning. The temptation, then, is to jump in the glider, have it pulled onto the runway, ask for connection to the tow plane, and GO. That would be a big mistake. One must proceed methodically. As one pilot friend remarked, "It's what you don't inspect that bites you." I raise the Plexiglas canopy by its forward hinge and reach back to turn on the valve of the oxygen bottle, which can't be reached in flight. I check that the oxygen pressure gauge on the instrument panel shows a full tank. I connect the hose of the oxygen mask to the bottle and put the mask on the seat. Later, it will sit on my lap when it's not over my face. Then I stow a sweater, a jacket, and two liters of water behind the seat, securely enough that they won't fly about in rough air. These will be needed if I end up spending the night in the desert. With some bungee cords, I secure the recording barograph on a small shelf behind the headrest, and turn it on. I listen to its ticks, and will listen again during the flight, just to reassure myself that I haven't made the horrid error of forgetting to turn it on.

That takes care of things that are out of reach during flight. Then I put a map in a narrow pocket on the left side of the cockpit. In the corresponding pocket on the right I put a package of Peanut M&M's and a package of cheese crackers. (At the end of the day, the cheese crackers had not been touched and a few M&Ms remained uneaten.) Low on the left, where it will be next to my left hip, I place a one-liter bottle of water for use during the flight. I plug in the microphone cable and put the microphone on the seat. Like the oxygen mask, it will rest on my lap. Then I check that the camera, mounted on the left side of the canopy, contains film and is sealed with a lead-clamped wire (as required by the Soaring Society of America).

Now it's time to get on board. Holding the microphone and oxygen mask, I lower myself into the seat and scoot an inch this way or an inch that way until I feel comfortable. I adjust the position of the rudder pedals to match the length of my legs. I fasten the lap and shoulder belts. I turn on the radio. Then I can survey my domain. Between my legs is the stick that controls the motion of the elevator and ailerons. Ahead of me on the instrument panel are an airspeed indicator, an altimeter, two vertical-speed indicators (they work in different ways and complement one another), an oxygen gauge, a clock, and a radio. Emerging from the panel are three cables attached to small wooden handles. Pulling the yellow handle releases the tow rope, thereby freeing the glider from its tow plane. Pulling the black handle releases a lock on the rudder pedals to permit adjustment for the length of the pilot's legs. Pulling the red handle—in an emergency only—pops loose the canopy so that the pilot can get out of the glider. Since I am not going to wear a parachute, this safety feature is of no value to me. I had weighed the extra security of a parachute against the discomfort of sitting on it all day, and opted for comfort. Finally, on the left side of the cockpit, near the instrument panel, are two handles. Pulling one of them retracts the landing gear. Pulling the other one opens the "spoilers," the panels extending from the wings to reduce lift and make it easier to descend rapidly. I used them that afternoon when Tony Sabino pointedly urged me to land.

Now I lower and latch the canopy, bringing the magnetic compass into view. I check that there are a couple of inches between the top of my head and the canopy, and cinch up the shoulder harness a bit tighter, so that turbulence won't cause head and Plexiglas to collide.

By this time, still on the ground, I am beginning to feel that the cockpit and I are a harmonious whole. The feeling is reinforced in the air. After I have settled into the rhythm of the day's flying, the cockpit itself becomes the universe. The glider doesn't move; the land and sky move. When I pull the stick to the left to lower the left wing, it seems that I have caused the horizon to tilt to the right while I remain sitting still. When I encounter sinking air, it seems that the land is rising toward me. When I approach a cloud, it seems that I sit motionless as the cloud approaches me. Small wonder that at the end of the day I was reluctant to leave the nest that the cockpit had become.

Profile

Bill Bullock
(1923-2005)

Photo courtesy of Judy Bullock

Once, when Bill Bullock's son David, then a teen, was wrestling with some minor crisis in his life, he went to his father and asked, "How do you know when to say no?" Bill, for whom aviation provided the context for addressing all issues, answered, "A good pilot always knows when to say no." David didn't tell me whether that answer helped him at the time, but he said that he often pondered it afterwards.

To say that being a good pilot is knowing when to say no may at first seem as fatuous as "Love means not ever having to say you're sorry." But it isn't. A good pilot knows when to say no to flying through a vicious line of thunderstorms, or to taking off when only one set of spark plugs is functioning correctly (each cylinder has two), or to inviting a friend to go up for a sightseeing flight just after downing a glass or two of wine, or to

173

descending into a box canyon with no certain assurance of being able to fly out of it, or to charging off into the night in order to get home when the forecast weather at the home airport and all potential alternates is below what the pilot and the plane can handle.

There are overcautious pilots who say no all the time—nervous Nellies who are spooked by strong wind or darkness or scattered thunderstorms. They don't get much joy from flying, and would be better off to say a permanent no to flying. Good pilots—the really good ones—know when to say yes as well as when to say no. Their log books are full of memorable flights, some exciting, but none crossing the line of unacceptable risk. Bill Bullock, in his career, flew deliberately into numerous thunderstorms and into the eyes of some hurricanes and across the Rockies in a small plane at night. He knew the capabilities of his planes and himself.

Bill soloed a Piper Cub in 1942, when he was 19. In 1992, at age 69, he stopped flying for pay. In fifty years and more than 13,000 hours of flying, he never damaged himself and never damaged an airplane—if you don't count dents from hailstones and scarred metal from lightning strikes. Bill's son David wonders if that 1992 decision to turn amateur was all part of knowing when to say no. Maybe Bill decided that he no longer met his own standards of performance, that the odds were no longer stacked in his favor.

*B*ill Bullock was born in Champaign, Illinois in 1923. He had his first airplane ride in 1938 as a high-school sophomore. He was treated to the ride by a friend. It cost a dollar. Writing much later for a high-school reunion report, Bill said matter-of-factly about that ride, "I had thought I wanted to be an aircraft pilot, and my interest continued." Typical Bullock. As plain-spoken, as free of embellishment, as it's possible to be. He did, indeed, become a pilot, flying for 63 years from his first solo in a J3 Cub in Wooster, Ohio to his last flight out of Peterson Air Force Base in Colorado Springs, Colorado, in 2005.

Bill graduated from University High School in Champaign in 1941, half a year before Pearl Harbor. He entered college that fall and completed a year of study before the inevitability of military service caught up with him. He chose the Navy and entered flight training. I say "chose" without knowing for sure how he got into the Navy. He may have enlisted before being drafted, or he may have been drafted and ended up in the Navy by preference or by chance. In any case, he found himself in flight training in Texas in 1942, which must have been very much to his liking. Yet he promptly flunked out (or "washed out," to use the military lingo). As he told it later, he had fallen and broken an elbow in a basketball game the day before a flight test. He went ahead with the test, trying, unsuccessfully, to make one hand do the work of two. I suspect that this steeled his resolve to become a pilot, and a good one.

Shifts from one service to another are not so common, although Tony Sabino managed it (see page 82), and so did Bill Bullock. Following the flight-test debacle in Texas, he arranged to be transferred to the Army Air Corps (before there was a separate Air Force). There, he was given triple-barreled training as a gunner, bombardier, and navigator. By the time he was designated a Navigator, and given the rank of Second Lieutenant (at the time, becoming an officer and a gentleman apparently required only a year of college), the war was nearly over. Bill stayed in the Army until 1947, practicing his craft of navigation on long flights in the western Pacific, touching down in Australia, China, Japan, and the Philippines.

Returning to his home town, Bill enrolled at the University of Illinois, earning a bachelor's degree in general engineering in 1950. Somehow he got in a lot of flying hours, for by 1949 he held not only a Pilot's license, but also a Flight Instructor's rating. Eventually he earned a multi-engine rating, a commercial license, an Airline Transport Pilot certificate, a glider license, and an A&P license.

Bill found time in college for romance, too. In June 1950, with the ink not yet dry on his bachelor's degree, he married Jean Davis Layson. Needless to say, aviation was a big part of their life together. Their son David, born in 1958, remembers flying here and there around the country with his parents when he was quite young, sometimes in a single-engine Beechcraft Bonanza, sometimes in a twin-engine plane. "We used planes the way other families used cars," he told me. I asked David how a struggling young family could afford such pricey planes. "It was his research company, ASTRO, that owned the planes," David explained. "They were as likely as not to have meteorology measuring equipment hanging from their wings."

Unfortunately David lost his mother to cancer in 1964, when he was only six. Except for one short and unsuccessful marriage after that, Bill remained unattached until he married twenty-seven-year-old Judy McPeak (thirty-four years his junior) in 1984. That final marriage, a happy one, lasted until Bill's death in 2005. When I interviewed Judy shortly after Bill's death, I could tell from all the detail she gave me about his early life that he had opened up his heart to her much more than he was inclined to do with others.

To encapsulate Bill Bullock in a single phrase, he was a weather pilot. In the 1950s he flew missions for the Illinois Water Survey to study the patterns of precipitation in that state. In the 1960s he flew missions for a pair of weather researchers, Charlie Moore of New Mexico Tech and Bernie Vonnegut (Kurt's brother) of the State University of New York at Albany. In the same decade he became chief of flight operations at the National Center for Atmospheric Research (NCAR) in Boulder, Colorado. In the 1970s he constructed the SPTVAR research plane for the Navy and flew it regularly into thunderstorms. In the 1970s and the 1980s he flew weather missions for NASA in and around Florida to help assess weather hazards for spacecraft launches from the Kennedy Space Center. That's where he tangled with some hurricanes. Along the way, to facilitate his weather

flying, he formed two companies: ASTRO, in Illinois, in
the 1960s, and AIRO, in Colorado, in the 1970s.

As if to emphasize—by contrast—the description of
Bill as a weather pilot, his resume includes this entry:
"1956, 3 months, First Officer [co-pilot], Ozark
Airlines." Bill preferred to be in charge of the airplanes
he flew, and evidently didn't take to flying in the right
seat. Later he became known for his prickly personality.
Everyone admired Bill's piloting skills, and admired his
willingness to charge into some of the world's worst
weather in search of more and better data. Not everyone
admired his insistence on doing things his way. Yet, over
the years, he taught innumerable students to fly or to fly
better. They must have seen what I saw, a talented guy
who was patient and helpful in the cockpit, who left his
belligerence on the ground.

I remember Bill at the Socorro, New Mexico airport,
meticulously inspecting measuring equipment that he
had helped to install on his beloved "Spitfire," meticulously sorting his Jeppesen charts*, meticulously making
entries in his log book. At one point in his later life, he
summarized in detail his flight experience. As of that
time, in 1995, he had accumulated 12,155 hours as
a pilot in addition to his 1,251 hours as a navigator. His
piloting time was divided among multi-engine planes

---

* Jeppesen charts are used for flying on instruments and making bad-weather
approaches. They need sorting because they are constantly being updated.
(Jeppesen is a private company based in Denver, where the founder, Elrey
Borge Jeppesen, started making and selling charts in the 1930s. He saved a lot
of lives then and is probably still saving them. The U.S. government also has
a chart service.)

(3,140 hours), single-engine planes (8,938 hours), and gliders (77 hours). I display these numbers only as a way of illustrating his care in record-keeping, not so common among high-time pilots. He also reported that more than half of his pilot-in-command time—6,621 hours, to be exact—was spent instructing. I'm not sure, but I suspect that he logged the two flights he made with me in other airplanes before turning me loose in the "Spitfire" as instruction time. He should have. They were good flights.

By the time Bill Bullock laid his hands on the Martin-Marietta 845 drone that was to become SPTVAR, it had already evolved substantially from its origin as a Schweizer 2-32 glider. The glider's three-person cockpit was gone. The ship now had an engine (a 200-horsepower Lycoming) and the necessary gas tanks and fuel lines. It had acquired a tricycle landing gear that raised the fuselage far enough off the ground to prevent the propeller from nicking the pavement or dirt. (The original glider had had a single small wheel protruding from its fuselage.) The plane's controls were managed by radio control from the ground. Actually, the Navy, which owned this drone, had lost several like it. These planes had the bad habit, when brought in for a landing, of sometimes going splat instead of touching down smoothly. Even this one had a banged-up nose from a hard landing in which the nose wheel had buckled, but it had been put back together, not scrapped.

This particular drone, scarred but serviceable, had been assigned to Charlie Moore at New Mexico Tech for use in thunderstorm research. It was sitting at the Socorro airport. When Charlie asked Bill Bullock if he would like to help instrument the drone and control its flights into thunderstorms from the ground, Bill had a better idea—to turn it into a piloted aircraft and then do what he liked doing best, flying into nasty weather himself. He no doubt divined, correctly, that he could control the plane better from inside it than from the ground, and do a better job of adjusting a flight plan to the reality of the weather if he were imbedded in the weather.

Charlie agreed and the Navy agreed. Bill's AIRO, Inc. was assigned the task of creating SPTVAR. The drone—with wings detached—was moved to a space provided by an equipment rental company in Littleton, Colorado, and later to a garage in Colorado Springs. In both places, the work space was tight. AIRO consisted, actually, of just a few people, including Bill's teen-age son David, who described himself as a gofer, although he was already skilled in metal work. The job took most of a year. David, whose hands were small as well as deft, was the one who had to take the parts of a disassembled pulley control box, shoe-horn them into the rear of the fuselage through a pair of small openings (inspection ports), and there re-assemble them.

In Littleton, the plane was cut in two just forward of the wings. Then twenty inches of new fuselage was added and the parts rejoined. The single-seat cockpit that was inserted had to have the usual stick, rudder pedals, throttle, fuel controls, electrical switches, and so on. Covering it was a bubble canopy of Plexiglas taken from a different glider.

There's no record of SPTVAR's first flight from Peterson Air Force Base. Bill Bullock had the right stuff. If I know him correctly, he made no big deal of it—just climbed in and took off, confident that a plane he had so lovingly designed and assembled would work as it should. I suspect it did. When I flew it later, it provided no surprises and no unexpected thrills. Once I was wedged into the cockpit, that is.

About that cockpit. When I interviewed Bill's son David in 2005, he confirmed for me what I had long suspected. "The entire cockpit was designed around my father's body specifications," he said. "There were drawings of him, his height, breadth, and so on." Bill told his associates at the time that he didn't want to waste space. It's just possible that he had something else in mind, to minimize the incentive for any other pilot to fly his lovely (even if ungainly) "Spitfire." As it turned out, he was gracious about letting me fly it, once he had determined by flying with me in a couple of other airplanes that I was a fairly acceptable pilot. I've always been happy that I met his standard.

-9-
Helping Out

On a Friday afternoon in late March 1982 the intercom in my office at New Mexico Tech buzzed. "It's Jerry Hoogerwerf," announced Lucy Chavez, my secretary. "Thanks. I'll take it," I said.

Jerry managed the Socorro airport at the time and was one of my flying buddies. He and his wife Sandra and their young daughter had arrived several years earlier from Albuquerque. Although I was old enough to qualify for membership in AARP, my romantic attachment to flying was so strong that I had trouble understanding why Jerry had settled in our out-of-the-way town instead of going for the glamour of an airline job. He had no interest in the so-called glamour. In Socorro he had no stripes on his sleeve and no peaked cap, but he could be home every night and, in the daytime, do what he liked to do—which was to fly airplanes, fix them, and give flight instruction. He also sold gas, collected hangar rent, answered the phone, and swept out the shack that served as office and lounge. The small income he pieced together at the airport, together with his wife's salary as a teacher, made ends meet.

On the phone Jerry came right to the point. "Ken, Leo Lujan needs to deliver a corpse to Lubbock on Sunday, and the weather forecast is not favorable. Would you be able to help him out? My plane is out of service right now, and there's no one else available who can fly on instruments." Leo Lujan was the local undertaker who doubled as County Coroner (he also served on the School Board and, if I recall correctly, worked part time as a pharmacist).

This wasn't the first time I had been called on to conduct an aerial mission in a good cause. Once three geologists from the Tech faculty came to me, excited because they had discovered a new fault down toward Truth or Consequences. Could I fly them down so they could look at it from above and take pictures? Certainly, I said. The reconnaissance was successful, even if I couldn't oblige their request that I fly even more slowly than eighty miles per hour as we circled the site. As always on such missions, I asked only that I be reimbursed for the cost of gas.

Another time, a rancher drove up to the operations shack at the Socorro airport in a state of some agitation. Some of his cattle were missing. He thought they had been rustled, and he had a pretty good idea who might have done it. I happened to be there, and Jerry was busy, so he suggested I fly the mission. Borrowing Jerry's Cessna 172, smaller and slower than my Bonanza and thus more suited to search for cattle rustlers, I flew the rancher to survey the countryside northwest of Bernardo (a crossroads twenty-five miles north of Socorro). He told me he would recognize his cattle for sure because they had unusual coloration. We covered the territory thoroughly, flying low and slow, but without success. The cattle turned up on their own a few days later. (This kind of flying takes careful attention to what one is doing. There's a standard story among pilots. A wife, concerned for her pilot husband's safety, says to him as he's leaving for the airport, "Remember, dear, fly low and slow." She could not give worse advice. Flying slow invites an inadvertent stall, and if that happens while flying low, there's no way out. Lives have been lost to flying low and slow.*)

One of the people I most enjoyed helping out was Sonny Baca, the County Sheriff. Now and then he needed to pick up or deliver prisoners in other towns. Sonny was Gary Cooper with a Spanish accent and a dry wit. He was tall and lean and probably slept in his cowboy boots. These missions with Sonny made me uneasy only once, when we went to Santa Fe to collect a bare-footed, tousle-haired prisoner with eyes darting in every direction. He was accompanied by a psychiatric nurse. On other flights, with only three of us on board, Sonny sat in back with the prisoner. This time he sat up front, feigning a lack of concern, and the nurse sat in back with

---

* This story has "legs." Dozens of times over the years, as I was leaving the house headed for the airport, I said to my wife, "Don't worry, dear, I'll fly low and slow." One must wonder whether the wife in the original story had her own reasons for what she advised.

the prisoner. I couldn't tell for sure, but the look this prisoner gave me when we arrived in Socorro made me think he enjoyed the flight. Maybe he was just relieved that it was over.

*B*ut this call from Jerry was the first time I had been asked to carry a dear departed from one place to another.

I didn't need to think very long. "Sure," I said, "I'll be glad to do it. But it will have to be in the afternoon, because I've promised to fly Owen Lopez from Albuquerque to Ruidoso on Sunday morning." Owen, although a bit shaken by the icing experience in the Mooney, was still happy to fly with me.

"That should work," said Jerry. "I'll check with Leo. I can take the right front seat out of your plane after you get back from your morning flight, so there will be room for the corpse."

"Sounds good," I said.

"And by the way," said Jerry, "just for fun, may I come along as a passenger on your morning flight to Albuquerque and Ruidoso?"

"That would be great," I said. Jerry probably enjoyed flying into Albuquerque and Ruidoso for the same reasons I did: Albuquerque because you were sneaking in amidst commercial and military traffic and got treated like one of the big boys, Ruidoso because it offered a challenging short strip nestled in the mountains.

Our Sunday morning flight was smooth and beautiful. The heavy weather was farther east, along the New Mexico-Texas border and into West Texas. While I went home for lunch, Jerry set to work removing the seat from my plane. When I got back to the airport, that job was done. Leo showed up in his hearse, and we carefully loaded the corpse (inside two body bags) into my plane, with its head forward, opposite my feet, and with its feet tucked under the right rear seat. (My Beechcraft Bonanza had one engine, two seats up front, two rear seats, and a small child's bench behind the rear seat, making it a six-seater if the passengers were chosen carefully enough.) Leo put a wooden block under the corpse's head and explained to me the importance of keeping the head elevated so that no bodily fluids leaked out. I was more than happy to cooperate with this instruction.

For some reason I was too diffident to ask Leo about his corpse—who it was, why it had to go to Lubbock. I assumed that some Texan had wandered into New Mexico and died there, and then, like other Texans, was encouraged to go back home. In Ruidoso, whose gorgeous ski slopes were sometimes crowded with Texans, one could see bumper stickers on pickups offering wisdom such as "If God had wanted Texans to ski, He would have put mountains in Texas," or, more succinctly, "Ski Lubbock." (To appreciate the latter sentiment, you have to know that there are no hills anywhere near Lubbock.)

Indeed, when we reached eastern New Mexico, the weather got rough. I picked up an instrument clearance by radio and entered the clouds. My passenger didn't seem to mind the bumps. I made an instrument approach into Lubbock and taxied to the parking area for transient planes. Right on schedule, a polished black hearse drove up, and two teen-aged boys got out, dressed for the occasion in black suits, white shirts, and muted ties that bespoke their calling.

We carefully unloaded the corpse, keeping the head elevated.

"I have to take back the body bag," I said. They both looked alarmed.

"It's OK. There's another bag inside the outer one." Thus reassured, they unzipped the outer bag and we tossed it into my airplane.

Both boys were eyeing my plane, and I answered their questions about it: How fast did it fly? How high? Where did I fly it? Did I need oxygen? Then one of them, no doubt envisioning a new career, asked, "Is this what you do for a living?"

"Only on weekends," I answered.

M ost of the people I ferried around were alive. When I lived in the Boston area and flew out of Bedford's Hanscom Field, a joint military-civilian airport not far from Concord, I learned that the Boston University FM station broadcast a sort of bulletin board for people offering or seeking rides. One could hear things like "Driving to Indianapolis, leaving next Thursday, room for two," or "I'm looking for a ride to Virginia on Saturday." I suspect that my notices may have been the first concerned with travel by air. Now and then, when I had a trip scheduled and had room for passengers, I used this outlet to let the Boston community (meaning, mainly, its hordes of university students) know. As often as not, someone would sign up, letting me do a favor to a young person in exchange for a small contribution toward my expenses.

On one flight, we were barely off the ground when my passenger, evidently excited by the whole experience, told me that there was something he had forgotten to do before we left, and that the need was now urgent. I landed at the next available small field—Orange, Massachusetts, I think—pulled off on a taxiway near the end of the runway, stopped, and let him hop out to relieve himself. The rest of the trip went fine.

On another trip, a valuable bit of cargo had to be jettisoned. I had two passengers, a young man going to Toronto, and a young woman headed for Detroit, which was my destination, too. I filed the necessary flight plans and off we went, in a Cessna 172. The young man disembarked in Toronto, as planned, and the young woman moved up to the front seat to continue on to Detroit. Somewhere along the way, I mentioned to her that because we had stopped in Canada, we would need to clear Customs in Detroit, and for that reason would land at the international airport, Detroit Metro, rather than the airport closer to town, Detroit City. She looked alarmed. "Will they go through my luggage?" she asked.

"Possibly," I said "You can't predict."

"How about my purse? Will they look at that?"

"Perhaps. Given your age, it's even likely."

"Oh, how terrible. I'm bringing my boyfriend a gift,

the finest hash I could find. What can we do? Can you hide it?"

I told her that I was not willing to hide it in the plane and that, unless she wanted to take quite a chance, she had better get rid of it. The idea distressed her mightily, but she decided to follow my advice. I slowed to about 65 miles per hour and out came a canister from her purse. I opened the window on my side (on a 172, it is hinged on top and swings out) and we consigned the hash to a watery grave. By that time we were over Lake St. Clair just east of Detroit, so no lucky Canadian was going to find her treasure.

In Detroit, the Customs agent must have judged her to be all sweet innocence, and must have decided that I, too, was no threat to the nation. He stamped a form and waved us through without inspecting anything.

After moving to New Mexico, I decided to continue the practice of offering rides to students (except not those from my own university). It was mutually beneficial. The student got where he or she wanted to go for a small cost, I got a little help with my expenses, and we had some old-young companionship along the way. The University of New Mexico, like Boston University, had a radio ride board on its FM station, and I used it from time to time. One young woman, named Hedy, whom I flew from Santa Fe to Baltimore (with rest stops in Joplin, Missouri and Lexington, Kentucky—stops worth making just to drink in the local accents), was so enthralled with the experience that she signed on to fly round trip from Santa Fe to San Francisco with me and my wife some months later. On that latter trip, taken in January, we landed en route at Grand Canyon, excruciatingly beautiful after a fresh snowfall, and at a balmy Death Valley, where the altimeter wound down below zero feet in the approach for landing. From Death Valley it's quite a climb to get up and over the Sierras, passing close to Mount Whitney, the highest peak in the Lower 48. Approaching San Francisco, the controller wanted me to fly as fast as possible. I did my best, and watched an airliner nevertheless edge past me as we angled down in parallel approaches. On the ground, I discovered that the changes in altitude and air pressure had been more than a bottle of ink I had brought along could stand. It had made quite a mess of my brief case.

And then there were Don, Elizabeth, Carol, and Mollie. Don Salmon was New Mexico Tech's Director of Development. He was headed to Hartford, Connecticut, and I to the Boston area. Using UNM's radio ride board, I had advertised two available seats to the east. Elizabeth and Carol signed up. They wanted to go to Pennsylvania: Carol to Pittsburgh and Elizabeth to Allentown. Their destinations were on our way. Since it looked like it was going to be a long day—probably at least twelve hours in the air and another four hours or so spent at stops en route (all this plus two hours lost to a time change)— I wanted to get an early start. We arranged to pick up Carol and Elizabeth at Mountainair at dawn. Mountainair, a short hop northeast of Socorro, has a long, smooth dirt strip at an elevation of 6,492 feet.

When Don and I took off from Socorro, it was still dark. We touched down at Mountainair at first light. Sure enough, as we taxied to a stop and shut off the engine, a pickup truck rolled up, driven, evidently, by a friend of the young ladies. Carol and Elizabeth bounded from the truck, as did their rather sizeable dog Mollie. The back of the pickup was filled with backpacks, suitcases, and other gear. As my prospective passengers explained to me, they were moving back east and had to take all their belongings—plus their dog—with them. My Bonanza, I told them, is roomy, but not that roomy; it's husky, but not that husky. We negotiated. Mollie, it turned out, was not negotiable. She had to go.

As Don looked on, bemused, I said to Carol and Elizabeth, "I'm willing to take off a little over gross weight, but not a lot over gross weight." We agreed that Mollie could go, that we would stuff the baggage compartment with whatever luggage they most needed, and that their friend would ship the rest to them. We got off without incident. Although the heavily loaded Bonanza didn't exactly climb like a rocket, it had no difficulty making its way expeditiously to cruising altitude. Mollie, sitting on Elizabeth's lap, appreciatively licked the back of Don's neck.

All on board were ready to get out and stretch (or bound about) at our rest stops in Tulsa, Oklahoma, and Bloomington, Indiana. As is typical on such flights, our nourishment was provided by vending machines. I picked Bloomington for a gas stop for old time's sake, and was able to greet my old friend John Myers. We dropped Carol and some luggage at Pittsburgh

International, then unloaded Elizabeth, Mollie and the rest of the luggage in Allentown. After delivering Don to Bradley field near Hartford, I took off, feather light, for the final hop to Bedford, Massachusetts, where I arrived around midnight.

*P*ilots can be loners, but, like nearly everyone else, they need peer groups. One of the informal organizations open to pilots is the Mile-High Club. To be considered for membership, a pilot must have engaged in cross-gender coupling while flying a plane more than 5,280 feet above the ground. Not having personally applied for membership, I am not familiar with all the rules—for instance, whether use of an autopilot is permitted or whether the qualifying activity must be completed while the pilot is in control of the airplane. I myself joined only AOPA (Aircraft Owners and Pilots Association) and SSA (Soaring Society of America), organizations that ask for no demonstrated achievements in the air.

$\mathcal{P}rofile$

Jerry Hoogerwerf

Photo courtesy of Jerry Hoogerwerf

*I*n 1987, Jerry Hoogerwerf bought a Cessna 205, an airplane that had rolled out of the Cessna factory in Wichita, Kansas nearly twenty-five years earlier. As this plane approaches its fiftieth birthday (and as Jerry edges toward his seventieth), there is no sign that they plan to part company any time soon. "It's just a perfect airplane for what I do," Jerry told me. "It's got a high wing, so my passengers and I can see down. It will fly slowly, which I sometimes need to do. It will carry a good load. And it doesn't cost too much to run."

What Jerry does, mostly, these days, is "environmental flying." He does forest surveys (the day after I interviewed him in 2005, he was going out to look for bark damage on piñon pines), fish surveys, wildlife surveys, and migrating bird surveys, usually in New Mexico, but sometimes in a neighboring state or in Mexico. On one of these flights, which can last up to six-

193

and-a-half hours, he is likely to have one or more scientists or officials of the Bureau of Reclamation or the Fish and Wildlife Service on board, armed mostly with their own eyes and cameras (and clip boards). Sometimes they use radios to monitor tagged animals.

Ever since he was fresh out of college and a Peace Corps volunteer in Costa Rica, Jerry has wanted to do his bit for humankind on this fragile Earth. Now he blends his love of flying and his love of environmental preservation, and makes a living at it. Not bad. Jerry is a happy man.

Jerry has flown more than 14,000 hours since he started flying seriously in 1973, at the age of thirty (I mention his age because most people who devote their lives to flying start earlier). Six thousand of those hours have been logged in his Cessna 205. That's more than three hundred hours per year—actually about the same time that an average driver sits at the wheel of a car in a year. This Cessna has fixed landing gear, which cuts down on maintenance costs. Having the gear hanging out keeps the plane from being a rocket, but Jerry is in no hurry. A 260-horsepower engine pushes it across New Mexico's deserts and mountains at 150 miles per hour, a modest speed for an airplane but twice the speed limit on Interstates 25 and 40, the highways that carve New Mexico into quadrants below. If Jerry wants to save gas, he slows to about 120 mph, and if he wants to have a good look at what's on the ground, he can putter along at 80. The 205 has six seats (including that of the pilot). With the fuel tanks filled, it can carry about 1,000 pounds—six people averaging

170 pounds unencumbered with luggage, or, more likely, fewer people plus luggage, equipment, and survival gear.

Jerry's 205 is a single-engine airplane with two engines. At any one time, one engine is bolted onto the airplane, providing the motive power, and the other one is sitting in Jerry's shop at the Socorro airport, either about to be overhauled, or in the middle of being over-hauled, or having just been overhauled. About once every four years, Jerry, who is a licensed aircraft mechanic as well as pilot, removes one engine, installs the other one, and starts the cycle anew.

erry was born in 1942 in Detroit, Michigan, the first of two sons (and two future pilots) born to Clarence (Klaus) and Gertrude Hoogerwerf. His father was a factory manager for Ford Motor Company. In 1949, Clarence was transferred to Ford International, and the family began an international saga. Jerry lived six months in France, then four years in Argentina, then five years in the Netherlands. He didn't return to America until 1960, when he enrolled as a freshman at Albion College in Michigan, having graduated from a Dutch high school. Of the languages Jerry acquired along the way, only Spanish has stuck, and it's useful to him now.

The family's 1949 flight to Paris in a TWA Lockheed Constellation was the first time that Jerry, then seven, and his brother Jim, then five, had been off the ground, and both of them say it was that flight that triggered their interest in aviation. "I stayed awake all night looking out at the big radial engines spewing this red-hot exhaust gas," Jerry told me. "After that my brother and I started making model airplanes and we started thinking about airplanes." Jim went on to become an airline pilot, retiring in 2005 after twenty-nine years with Delta Airlines.

While a freshman at Albion, Jerry went over to nearby Jackson, Michigan and paid for a flying lesson. But he couldn't afford to continue. For the next nine years, flying remained a dream, not a reality. First four years of college, then a year pinching pennies as a graduate student at Wayne State University near Detroit, then a year traveling and holding short-term jobs, then two years in the Peace Corps, serving in Costa Rica, then a year as a social worker at the Cuban Refugee Assistance Program in Miami, Florida. Finally, in 1969, Jerry, with the help of a scholarship and some savings, enrolled in graduate school at the University of Miami and tried flying again. He also got married. His bride, Sandra Henning, whom he had met at the Cuban Refugee Assistance Program, was, in his words, a "white-knuckle flier." After soloing, Jerry put flying on hold again.

The new couple also put their honeymoon on hold, waiting a year until Jerry earned his master's degree in Latin American Studies. Then they took a protracted automobile trip across America, Mexico, and Central America. No airplanes.

But the itch was still there. After Jerry and Sandra moved to Albuquerque in 1972 and he opened a Volkswagen repair shop (she worked with children in a pre-school), he began to cast his eye toward Kirtland

Air Force base, the big joint military-civilian airport on the south side of town. In 1973, he resumed his flying lessons there, and soon had his private pilot's license. Within a few years, he had earned his commercial license, instrument rating, and instructor's license (and also acquired a daughter Tanya, born in 1974). With the instructor's certificate in hand, he began teaching students to fly, and he loved it. Soon he was spending more time in the air and less in the Volkswagen garage. By 1977, he left four-wheeled vehicles behind and was instructing full time, both in Albuquerque and in Belen, about thirty miles to the south.

In Albuquerque, Jerry joined a group calling itself Duke City Aviation that owned several small planes used for rental and for giving instruction. When he wasn't instructing, he was likely to be flying off somewhere in the West with friends for fun, including trips to Montana and California (it's called building time). At Belen's Mid Valley Airport, he also began to work toward becoming a licensed aircraft mechanic.

In 1978, sponsored by the Mid-Valley flight school where he worked, Jerry entered a Precision Flying Tournament organized by Cessna Aircraft Company. He flew a Cessna 150, a two-place plane, the smallest plane that Cessna made. There were three tasks. The first was to approach and land without power (engine idling), touching down beyond a line on the runway but as close as possible to it. Landing short of the line was disqualifying. The second task was to prepare a detailed flight plan with projected times over a set of check points on the ground. The third task was to fly that route and try to nail the times of arrival over the checkpoints. Observers on the ground checked the times of the competing airplanes passing overhead.

Jerry won the local contest in Albuquerque. He went on to win the western regional contest, also held in Albuquerque. Then he went on to the nationals, competing in Kansas (Cessna's home turf) against the winners of all the other regional contests. Jerry won that, too. Quite an achievement, especially in a Cessna 150, which, because of its slow speed, is more vulnerable to winds than are faster planes. And there's no after burner to kick in if you have fallen behind your schedule. Jerry described the tournament to me in his quiet, understated way, and then added, with a small smile, "The prize was a thousand dollars and a huge trophy so I was pretty proud of that."

I n 1979 Jerry moved with Sandra and Tanya seventy-five miles south to Socorro to take a job at the college (where I was president at the time) and, at the same time, to co-manage the local airport with a friend, Richard Reese. Jerry's job at the college was with a division that did mostly military-related work. This division made use of the huge, uninhabited acreage adjoining the campus (and owned by the school) to blow things up. Because he now had his A&P license, Jerry could expertly assess damage to aircraft and aircraft parts resulting from firing various kinds of weapons at them. Still, it was working for someone else, which made Jerry restless.

When, the next year, his friend Richard Reese decided to leave town, Jerry quit the job at the college and became the airport's full-time manager. Within a year or so, he had upgraded his instructor's certificate to allow him to give instrument training, and also, with the help of a quickie course in Florida, he had earned his multi-engine rating.

Fortunately, because of Sandra's job in the local school, Jerry didn't need to be assured of a princely income. The city paid him its standard two hundred dollars per month. Beyond that, he kept the profit from selling gas and kept overnight tie-down fees as well as half the income from hangar rental. He taught students, rented airplanes, and did charter flying for college officials and local business people. He did some aircraft maintenance, and, for a while, bought and sold air-planes—planes that, in real-estate parlance, were fixer uppers. So a little here and a little there. Enough to get by. Jerry was happily independent again. "Rarely in my life have I worked for anyone else," Jerry told me. "In Socorro, I was doing exactly what I wanted to do. I was working for myself and I was working in aviation, the field I had decided I wanted to be in."

Still, he had the nagging feeling that he ought to have an assured steady income as he moved into middle age. So, in 1985, at age 43, he took a job as a co-pilot with Mesa Airlines, a western regional carrier that flew twin-turbo-prop planes. He stuck with it for six months. Mesa, like most small regional airlines, knew that it didn't have to pay well or provide many perks because there was no shortage of pilots wanting to get a start in the airline industry, pilots for whom the chance to wear a uniform and build time in turbine-powered aircraft was recompense enough, if it was a steppingstone to United, American, Delta, Continental, or Northwest. Jerry was paid $850 per month, and, when away from home, was put up in trailers, fire houses, or cheap motels two to a room.

That's the last time Jerry worked for someone else. His airport manager job was waiting for him when he left Mesa and he came back to Socorro to stay.

About that time, New Mexico Tech acquired a surplus Baron, a sleek twin-engine Beechcraft, for which the military had no further need. Jerry did a little work on it and then used it to ferry college officials around the state. Once, approaching Santa Fe with W. Dennis Peterson, Tech's financial vice president, on board, Jerry pushed the lever to lower the landing gear and nothing happened. Denny Peterson, as I knew from personal experience, believed that God had not intended humans to fly (he had been my reluctant passenger a couple of times when he just had to get somewhere quickly). Now, sitting next to Jerry, he began to envision the possible outcomes of landing with the gear up. It was a busy time of the year. He couldn't really spare the time for an extended hospital stay.

Jerry was calm. He pulled out the operations manual, read the section entitled "What to do if the landing gear doesn't go down" (or some such heading), and asked Denny to find the crank in the back seat and turn it seventy-five times. "I found the crank," Denny told me, "turned it seventy-five times, and returned to my seat and buckled up." The control tower was unmanned at the time, so there was no one to look at the plane as it flew by and say whether the gear was really down. Jerry decided that it was, and landed—cautiously. Crunch. Tires met pavement, and nothing gave way. When they had taxied to the parking area and shut down the engines, Jerry asked Denny if he should wait and fly him back to Socorro. "I wanted to kiss the earth," Denny told me. "I had had enough of flying for the moment. I told Jerry to check the plane and head home if he thought it was safe to do so. I found ground transportation when my meeting ended."

The Baron misbehaved one other time. The passenger on that occasion was the CEO of the Aerojet Corporation, who was by chance a former test pilot. When the left engine failed because of a loss of oil pressure on the way into Albuquerque, Jerry shut it down, feathered the prop,* and landed without incident while his unfazed passenger showed not the slightest concern. The right stuff, I guess. After owning the Baron for only a few years, the college decided that it didn't need it after all.

As it turns out, in his 14,000-plus hours of flying, Jerry has never injured an airplane, a passenger, or himself.

---

* To "feather" a prop is to rotate its blades to that they line up with the direction the plane is moving. In that position they slice into the wind like a knife through butter and offer the least resistance.

*S*oon after Jerry bought his Cessna 205, he learned about an organization called Light Hawk, which uses volunteer pilots and their airplanes for environmental missions, at that time in the western United States. "They were trying to start a program in Central America," Jerry told me, "and they were looking for a pilot with an airplane who would want to volunteer to go down there. When I saw that, I thought this is just perfect. I speak Spanish, I've been to Central America, I have an airplane, I'm a pilot. So I volunteered and flew down to Costa Rica. I carried people who were taking pictures of areas that maybe needed protection. Light Hawk did a lot of surveys: wildlife surveys, land and forest surveys, and fish surveys. That was exciting. I started volunteering every year after that, sometimes several times a year." Light Hawk reimburses Jerry for his direct expenses, and on a few occasions has provided a stipend as well.

Jerry soon learned that he could make a career of environmental flying. There turned out to be quite a demand for this sort of flying from government agencies willing to pay. Gradually, over the years, Jerry cut back on instructing and aircraft maintenance, and then relinquished the airport management to someone else. Now environmental flying is about all he does. Regrettably, fear of litigation has played a role in his getting out of instruction and maintenance. "I loved instructing," Jerry told me. "There's a great deal of satisfaction in seeing somebody start from ground zero and a few months later they're flying an airplane by themselves. I never had a student do more than minor damage to an airplane. Still, you worry. There's not much that insurance can do to cover a flight instructor. When you're young and you don't have anything, you don't worry about that sort of thing, but when you get older and you have some things that you don't want to lose, you don't want to take undue risk." The same reasoning, Jerry told me, applies to working on other people's airplanes.

*J*erry's flying genes may not have got passed on, but his environmental and humanitarian ones did. After his daughter Tanya graduated from New Mexico Tech in 1997 with a degree in environmental engineering, she joined the Peace Corps and went to El Salvador. She also spent time in Uruguay, and in late 2005 was in Sri Lanka helping the victims of the tsunami. Her preferred method of getting around is on the ground. She rode trains all over Mexico, hitchhiked around Ireland, and once rode a bicycle from Denmark to Spain. She flies with her dad when it's the handiest way to get from A to B.

"What do you do when you aren't flying or planning a flight or working on airplanes?" I asked Jerry. "Well," he answered, "I read a lot. I just finished this great book. Here, I'll loan it to you." I took it and read it. It was the memoir of an airline pilot whose idea of fun was to cut the power on his Boeing 747 jet engines back to idle at thirty thousand feet, then glide to a landing with a load of passengers. The author had retired after an accident-free career.

Jerry's passion for flying isn't visible on the surface. But when I asked him if, during the winter months when there was a lull in environmental flying, he ever got the itch to go out and fly for fun, he said. "Oh, I do, all the time. I have an old Cardinal [another Cessna] that I keep out there and I just go. Yeah, if I don't fly for a few days I've just gotta go out and fly."

-10-
Making It

The Minden-Tahoe Airport sits at an elevation of 4,718 feet in Nevada's Carson Valley. As gliderports go, it is large. One of its three paved runways is long enough to accommodate jets. A second one is used mainly by gliders. The third one, rather neglected and with weeds growing up through its macadam, is partly a glider parking lot and partly an emergency strip to be used when the wind is howling down its length or when things get so busy that a glider needs an alternate place to land. A dirt strip parallel to one of the paved runways is used by landing tow planes and by the occasional glider when the parallel runway is otherwise tied up.

Minden-Tahoe used to have enough glider activity to keep two glider operations in business: Soar Minden and High Country Soaring. Somewhat by chance, I picked Tony Sabino's Soar Minden to help me toward a diamond badge. Tony is the only glider operator now. High Country Soaring went out of business in 2004, driven by a downturn in business and by friction with airport management. The downturn in business was one more unfortunate consequence of terrorism. Foreign pilots had been a mainstay of High Country's business (and are still an important part of Soar Minden's). After 9/11, many of them were finding it to be just too big a hassle and too long a wait to get visas to come and soar in America. As to the airport management, it seems that they were more interested in promoting bizjet activity than in supporting soaring, and found ways to make life hard for the soaring organizations. An odd state of affairs, given that Minden-Tahoe is a leading center for soaring, attracting pilots from all over the world—something, one would think, of which local officials should be inordinately proud. As I mentioned in my profile of Tony, he oversaw about 5,000 glider flights per year when he had competition. That number will no doubt rise. Minden-Tahoe could well be the busiest gliderport in the country. As for Tony, he is too stubborn and determined to be chased away after eighteen years of building a superb operation.

Since there aren't enough powered planes flying in and out of the airport to justify a control tower, communication by all traffic is on what's called a unicom frequency. On this frequency (122.8 megahertz), pilots announce their location and intentions, and get advisories from someone on the ground. A separate frequency (123.3 megahertz, which I mentioned before) is reserved for gliders. Glider pilots use it when they are away from the airport to talk to one another or to the home office. The day I landed at the US Marine Corps Sweetwater dirt strip, that's the frequency I used to reach a glider in the air and relay my earthbound location to Tony Sabino back at Soar Minden.

The Carson Valley, with an average elevation of about 5,000 feet, extends southward from Carson City, the state capital, for about 25 miles until it turns into the lumpy foothills of the Sierras. In an east-west direction, it is narrower—about 15 miles. To the east, it runs into the Pine Nut Mountains, modest by western standards, the highest peak of the Pine Nuts being at 9,451 feet. The Valley's western boundary is sharply edged by a north-south spur of the Sierras, whose highest points also reach above 9,000 feet. This spur is, in effect, a dam holding back Lake Tahoe, whose surface lies at an elevation of 6,229 feet. It's easy to see why this strikingly beautiful lake, hemmed in all around by mountains, is a tourist magnet winter and summer.

For a glider pilot trying to go somewhere from Minden-Tahoe, the first task is to get out of the valley. A distance flight begins when the glider pilot releases from the tow plane directly over the airport at no more than 3,000 feet above it. He or she then "notches the barograph." This means that the pilot dives the glider about two hundred feet before seeking to gain altitude, so that the trace left by the barograph needle, after rising steadily and briskly during the tow, shows a sharp little dip of decreasing altitude (a "notch"), indicating that the glider is no longer being towed. Now what comes next, I'll put in personal terms. If I have the good fortune to release in lift, I roll into a right turn and try to circle my way higher in a thermal. If I do not release in lift, I point the glider toward the Pine Nut Mountains and cruise in search of a thermal. If the lift I find is weak, I don't stay with it very long. Time is everything, and I am trying to cover ground. If the lift is strong, I ride it higher, gaining perhaps 2,000 feet before heading further eastward.

In the first part of the flight, I want to stay within gliding range of the airport. So if I am not very high, I dare not venture very far away. If I gain more altitude, I can venture farther. My goal is to be at 10,000 feet or higher when I reach the Pine Nuts. For several reasons, the lift there is likely to be better than over the valley. Its exposed rocks, some of them tilted toward the morning sun, heat up faster than the valley floor and trigger thermals that come earlier and are stronger. Because the base of the thermal is at elevated altitude, the top is also higher. Once secure above 10,000 feet, I try to ride still higher as I cruise southward along the mountain range. Only then do I cut the umbilical cord to the home airport. From here on, I have to be prepared for the possibility of landing somewhere else. Then it's upward, downward, and onward for hours to come.

When lift over the valley is anemic, getting started on a distance flight can be time consuming and frustrating. Once I literally spent more than five hours trying to get out of the valley. After an hour and a half, I knew I wasn't destined to cover any great distance that day, but I still wanted to break loose to see if I could fly a hundred miles or so. Here's how it goes. I gain a little altitude. I cruise eastward in search of more lift and don't find any. I turn back so that, if necessary, I can land back at the airport ("relighting," it's called). I find some weak lift near the airport. It saves me from relighting. I climb a thousand feet in it and head east again—or perhaps in a slightly different direction than before. I get some more weak lift, I ease farther from the airport, maybe five or six miles away. Then the lift gives out and I must turn back to avoid the possible embarrassment of landing on one of the little dirt strips east of the airport, or even in a farm field. And so on. Up a little, east a little, and back. I'm sure a more skilled pilot, with the sixth sense gained in countless hours aloft and with a willingness to stretch to the absolute limit how far he dare go before turning back, would be long gone and on his way. I try, I stretch, but I don't have that level of skill. I console myself with the thought that there are days when *no one* can stay up or cover ground. (And there are other days, as one friend put it, when you could cover ground strapped to a piece of plywood.)

On the July day in 1996 when I finally completed a 500-kilometer flight, I got out of the valley in about half an hour, found lift over the Pine Nuts, and left the southern end of that small mountain range at 12,000 feet. The experts say it's best to be at 15,000 feet at that point, because there's a lot of uncertain terrain ahead, but I had to settle for what nature offered that early in the day (about 1:00 p.m.) Thermals reach higher as the day goes on. Since there were no clouds to suggest where lift might be found, I had to take pot luck. I headed south toward Mount Patterson, twenty-five miles ahead. Mount Patterson, topping out at 11,673 feet, lies across the state line in California. It's a likely source of good lift.

My effort of the previous day had started in the same way, but Mount Patterson had not given me the traction I needed. After flirting with weak lift on its eastern and northern flanks, I had landed at the charmingly named Sweetwater Marine Corps air strip. I can hardly imagine a more beautiful place in which to sit and contemplate nature while awaiting help. The air at the strip's elevation of 6,868 feet was a pleasant 80 degrees or so, much cooler than back in the Carson Valley. There was a light breeze, the air was crystal clear, and there were meadows and mountains in view in every direction. I sat in wonder, munching my M&M's and sipping water, until, after an hour or so, the tow plane appeared. The tow out of Sweetwater offered only one unsettling surprise. The tow plane kicked up so much dust from the strip that for an instant I could see neither the tow plane nor the ground. I was inside a momentary cloud. All I could do was keep a light, firm grip on the stick and ease it back slowly, hoping the wings didn't tilt. Then I popped above the dust and all was well.

How many unsuccessful 500-kilometer attempts had I made? I can't say for sure, because some of them were so unpromising that I made no serious effort to complete the distance. Fourteen times, spread over more than a dozen years, I had completed all preparations, loaded the glider, and took off, mentally and physically prepared for a long afternoon. On six of those attempts I covered more than 250 kilometers, in times ranging from four-and-three-quarter to seven-and-three-quarter hours. (The flight that ended with the contemplation of nature in Sweetwater was not one of those six.) If you are an ace glider pilot reading these words, you will wonder at my ineptitude, since you have probably flown 500 kilometers in five hours, and probably more than once. Well, as I have said before, skill levels in flying gliders are not like those in driving cars or even in flying power planes. They are more to be compared with those that separate amateur athletes from the best professional ones. I am an earnest amateur.

My first effort, in May 1982, was actually the one that came closest to my goal. It was a "downwind dash" from Moriarty, New Mexico to a destination in Oklahoma a little more that 500 kilometers to the east. The Schweizer 1-26 I was flying is a low-performance glider much loved by pilots despite its modest capabilities, just as an old MG roadster might be beloved by auto enthusiasts despite the fact that it falls far short of a Porsche—or even a modern Chevrolet—in performance. I was not experienced enough and not aggressive enough. Despite reaching an altitude of 17,000 feet during the flight, I could tell as I slid past Amarillo in the late afternoon, faithfully following Interstate 40, that I was hardly likely to reach Oklahoma. That's the flight I described in Chapter 4 that ended in a pasture in White Deer, Texas.

Three years later, in June 1985, I spent nearly eight hours in the cockpit of a Grob 102, a medium-performance ship, only to land at the end of the afternoon at Luke Air Force Base # 1 west of Phoenix, after flying 380 kilometers from my starting point in Estrella, Arizona. The officer, whose welcome (cool, then warm) I described in Chapter 4, suggested that my first call be to the control tower of the active Air Force base closer to

Phoenix. I followed his advice. The controller was sympathetic, but said firmly, "You've got to be out of there by 8:00 a.m. We'll be conducting low-level simulated bombing runs at that time."

My second call was to Les Horvath at home. Unruffled, he promised to show up in a tow plane at 7:30 in the morning. After downing a hamburger and a soda and asking around the establishment where the officer had taken me, I found a very drunk patron ("I've been drinking since morning," he told me matter-of-factly) who agreed to drive me back to the air field, via a service station where I could buy a flashlight (there was one in the glider, but I had neglected to take it with me and it was now quite dark). My driver was barely able to stay within the confines of the two-lane road, which was blessedly free of other traffic. He dropped me at a gate in the fence around the field. Shining my light ahead of me, I walked as noisily as I could the mile to my glider, hoping that the light and the noise would encourage rattlesnakes to get out of my path. Sleeping in the cockpit—which felt like home anyway—was not bad at all, and, as I described earlier, Les showed up exactly on schedule as I was polishing off my breakfast of packaged cheese crackers and water.

$\mathcal{I}$ n these pages I have spoken of high altitudes and oxygen. Nearly every glider used for distance or wave flying carries an oxygen bottle, to which a mask can be connected. A regulator is constructed in such a way that oxygen flows only when the pilot has the mask on and breathes in, so there is no need to be turning the oxygen on and off during the flight. It's only necessary to don the mask or take it off as needed. My own rule is to put it on when going up through 13,000 feet and take it off when going down through the same altitude. Up to 15,000 or 16,000 feet, a pilot can still function reasonably well without oxygen, but performance and judgment may be somewhat degraded. It's best to be safe—and follow the law—by putting on the mask at no more than 14,000 feet. For a planned wave flight, it can make sense to put it on while still on the ground, so there's one less thing to think about in the air. (The Federal Air Regulation that I cited in Chapter 9 allows unlimited flying without oxygen below 12,500 feet and up to 30 minutes of flying without oxygen between 12,500 and 14,000 feet; it requires the use of oxygen above 14,000 feet.)

My only brush with hypoxia (insufficient oxygen) came in a wave flight near Lake Tahoe the day after I had achieved diamond altitude. Approaching 24,000 feet, I noticed that the windshield of the Grob began to appear frosty. I wasn't troubled, since it's common for frost to form on a windshield in the very cold temperatures aloft (probably somewhere between zero and 25 below that day), and one can always see out the side if forward visibility is impeded. Then, glancing down at the instrument panel, I noticed that it, too, appeared frosty. My brain was working well enough to tell me that the frost was in my head, not in the glider, and that the probable cause was lack of oxygen. I cinched the mask tighter and took a few deep breaths. The frost disappeared and the rest of the flight was uneventful.

From the southern end of the Pine Nuts, I made my way southward, successfully passing the Marine Corps strip at Sweetwater, and finding some good lift at Mount Patterson. "Don't leave Mount Patterson at less than 15,000 feet," Tony had said. "You'll need every foot of it. You may find some more lift on your way down to Potato Peak, but once you get to Mono Lake, it's all downhill to the Whites [the White Mountains] and there's no good place to land until you reach the cultivated fields." Tony was right. Fortunately, I did get to 15,000 feet, and indeed I needed it. From Mount Patterson to the cultivated fields nestled next to the northern end of the White Mountains is a run of about sixty miles, twenty of them over mountainous terrain, then forty miles over rough, forbidding desert country. In that sixty miles, tracking pretty much along the California-Nevada border, and circling only occasionally, I lost some 6,000 feet.

The Whites are an impressive if relatively small range that run north-south, edging the east side of the Owens Valley, with the even more majestic Sierras on the west side of the Valley. The highest peak of the Whites rises to over 14,000 feet, competitive with the best the Sierras have to offer. In the band just west of the Whites there is some farming, providing the cultivated fields Tony referred to (fields with the added advantage of being close to a highway). With about 3,000 feet of air separating me from these fields, I could breathe relatively easy and take the time to push a little farther east to explore the foothills of the Whites. Even though the cloudless sky provided no hint of where thermals might be, I was lucky enough to find one, then another, then another. It was mid-afternoon, and, as the local pilots say, the Whites were "working." Twice I came close to my legal limit of 18,000 feet as I worked my way south over the spine of the mountain range.

With altitude in the bank, I left the Whites to head further south toward my turnpoint, Tinnemaha Dam, about 25 miles south of the city of Bishop, California. With the dam off my left wing, I went far enough past it to catch it in the camera's sights as I banked steeply to the left a short distance south of the dam. When I rolled out of the bank headed northward after snapping three pictures, it was 4:00 o'clock and I was at 15,000 feet, halfway through my planned 500-kilometer flight. I had reason to be optimistic.

But I had a decision to make. Now there were some small cumulus clouds appearing over the Sierras, still none over the Whites. Should I head west to the Sierras, only ten or twelve miles away, and try to find my way home with the help those clouds might offer (a choice that would avoid the long desert crossing below Mt. Patterson), or should I head back northward to the Whites and try to retrace the route I had followed to get this far? I made the wrong decision. I went toward the Sierras. I was on a slowly descending elevator. No lift over the valley. No lift over the foothills of the Sierras (in fact, some sink because of down-wash off the mountains). When I reached a point a dozen miles west of Bishop, I was at an uncomfortable altitude of about 7,500 feet, scarcely 1,500 feet above the forests below. It looked like this was going to be just one more unsuccessful effort, and that my only chance of ending the day at an airport instead of in the boondocks was to turn east, go back across the Owens Valley, and land at Bishop.

I arrived over the Bishop airport about 1,100 feet above the ground, still having encountered no lift since Tinnemaha. "Well," I said to myself, "Nice try." I used a unicom frequency to contact someone on the ground and announced my intention to land. But I wasn't going to surrender until I had to. I eased a mile or two east of the airport to where some low hills began, keeping within gliding range of the airport. I encountered what glider pilots call "zero sink." It's actually very weak lift, just enough to allow the glider to fly level, neither gaining nor losing altitude. Heartened ever so slightly, I dared to fly just a bit farther east over the hills and toward the Whites. Miracle of miracles, I started going up. With the extra altitude, I could penetrate toward the foothills of the Whites. I was rewarded with strong lift.

I radioed the airport, said, in effect, "Never mind," and was on my way home. The faithful Whites propelled me back to nearly 18,000 feet, and I had no serious problems from there on. Three hours after leaving Tinnemaha, I arrived over the Minden-Tahoe Airport, a comfortable 3,000 feet above the ground, in no great hurry to land, with Tony urging me downward.

he Soaring Society of America numbers U.S. badges in the order they are awarded. Silver and gold badges date from the 1930s, diamond badges from 1950. John Robinson, a San Diegan and pioneer glider pilot, earned silver badge number 18 in 1937, gold badge number 2 in 1939, and diamond badge number 1 in 1950—the first in the world, not just in the U.S. (Robinson won various competitions and awards, designed a sensitive rate-of-climb instrument, improved the design of gliders, and was the first glider pilot to soar to high altitude in a wave. In his later years, he sported white sideburns that projected far enough from his face to provide a little extra aerodynamic stability.) As for me, I had earned silver badge number 3405 in 1977 and gold badge number 1304 in 1980. When Judy Ruprecht (who is known in the soaring fraternity as the "badge lady") notified me in 1999 that I had earned Diamond Badge number 858, she said, as I recall, "It must have been particularly satisfying to earn your Diamond Badge after so many years of trying." She was so right.

Soaring Society of America Diamond Achievement pin.

Afterword

ow did I come to choose the nine people profiled in these pages? They have not been featured in *Who's Who* and are unlikely candidates for the history books. They are just people I have met in my own flying odyssey who impressed me with their commitment to aviation and, above all, their style. They are "ordinary" people, but extraordinary in the ways they integrated their lives on the ground and in the air. In one way or another, each of them had an impact on my own pursuit of flying. Most important, I liked them. (I'm using the past tense here, but some are still flying and are still friends.)

Not surprisingly, half a dozen of the nine managed airports or airport operations, for that's where I met them—in Santa Fe, Bloomington, Socorro, Minden, and Estrella. Indeed, I met all nine at—where else?—airports. Four saw military service, although none was assigned flying as a principal military job. All were (or are) licensed power pilots, and more than half were (or are) licensed mechanics as well. Of the five who flew (or still fly) gliders, three strongly prefer to take to the sky without an engine. They all logged gobs of time in the air. Two tried airline work and then went back to private flying. One still flies big jets.

I salute these people and the many others—including Bob Buck—who helped to nurture my love affair with flying.

Acknowledgments

$\mathcal{I}$ am grateful to Chris Doig, Jerry Hoogerwerf, Les Horvath, Tony Sabino, Al Santilli, and Ray Smith— the six living persons profiled in these pages—for consenting to be interviewed and for sharing their stories with me. Tony Sabino's sons Tony, Jr. and Paul, his daughter-in-law Jamie Sabino, and his friend Sam Whiteside were also helpful. To learn more about the three persons no longer with us, I turned to their families and friends: Charlie Boyd's old friend Fred Duran and his step-daughter-in-law Mary Lou Montgomery; Bill Bullock's widow Judy and his son David; John Myers' sons Chuck and Dow and his widow June. All of these people kindly shared their recollections with me.

Mark Sellers flew me in his lovely Bellanca to visit with Bob Buck in Vermont. There Bob talked about his remarkable career, critiqued my manuscript, and introduced me to a most helpful writer, Kitty Werner, who provided a lot of sound advice on forming one's own publishing company.

Jerry Hoogerwerf, Jeff Nye, and Keith Richards read drafts of the book and provided useful advice. I thank them for that. People kind enough to provide an assortment of facts include Betsy Hershberg, Tom Knauff, Nancy Malmed, Joe O'Neill, Judy Ruprecht, and Tom Stowers.

This book is, in some ways, a family affair. My daughter Caroline Eisenhood checked facts and transcribed all of my interviews (plus two that she conducted herself). My son Adam served as both editor and designer. If the book looks good and reads well, it's because of his efforts. I thank my wife Joanne for her consistent encouragement and for sharing the sky with me on numerous occasions in both gliders and airplanes, including a couple of memorable transcontinental flights in four-seaters.

Left page — AIRCRAFT FLOWN / LOCAL OR CROSS COUNTRY

DATE 1953	MAKE OF AIRCRAFT	CERTIFICATE NUMBER	MAKE OF ENGINE AND H.P.	CLASS RATING	FROM	TO	SOLO DAY	N
7-7-53	Ercoupe	N93307	Cont 75		Local	Santa Fe		
7-16-53	"	"	"		"	"		
7-18-53	"	"	"		"	"		
"	"	"	"		"	"		
7-19-53	"	"	"		"	"		
7-28-53	"	"	"		"	"		
"	"	"	"		"	"		
8-1-53	"	"	"		"	"		
8-6-53	"	"	"		Santa Fe to albuq. and rt.			
8-8-53	"	"	"		Local			
11/1/53	Verner	N85376	C-65		Bmg.	Local		
					PAGE TOTAL			
					AMT. FORWARD			
					TOTAL TO DATE			

Right page — ROUTE OF FLIGHT / AIRCRAFT CATEGORY AND CLASS / INSTRUMENT

96	AIRCRAFT MAKE & MODEL	AIRCRAFT IDENT	FROM	TO	DURATION OF FLIGHT	RETRACT	MULTI ENGINE LAND	TAIL WHEEL	GLIDER	ACTUAL	SIMULATED (HOOD)	APPROACHES
6/30	LSA	45TH	MEV	MEV	3.8				3.8			
7/1	"	"	"	"	7.2				7.2			
7/4	C305A	5171G	Prv, Hld - PGC		0.2			0.2				
"	"	"	PGC	Local	0.5			0.5				
8/4	Scw 233	33986	"	"	0.3				0.3			
8/11	C305A	5171G	"	"	4.4			4.4				
9/4	"	"	PGC	PGC	0.7			0.7				
9/12	Scw 103H	11645	PGC	Local	0.4				0.4			
9/16	C305A	5171G	"	"	0.6			0.6				
10/6	C305A	5171G	"	"	1.4			1.4				
	NG Scw 104	1104 S	"	"	1.1				1.1			
	C305A	5171G	"	"	0.9			0.9				
					64.7	—	—	18.3	45.4	—	—	—
	C/n TD	1/1/76			4527.6	919.1	19.2	447.5	295.0	493.4	156.4	585
			PAGE TOTALS		4527.6							585
			PREVIOUS TOTALS									
THIS RECORD IS CERTIFIED TRUE AND CORRECT			NEW TOTALS									

PILOT'S SIGNATURE   K W Ford

222

Log Book #1, showing first flight in Ercoupe with Charlie Boyd, July 3, 1953

Log Book #7, showing Diamond Distance flight in LS-4, July 1, 1996

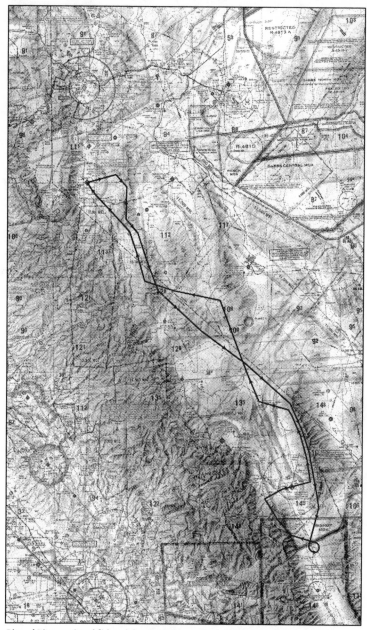

Diamond Distance estimated flight path from Soar Minden to Tinnemaha Dam and back, July 1, 1996

With Cessna 172, Provincetown, Massachusetts, September 1962

Philadelphia Glider Club (PGC), Bucks County, PA, July, 1985

My daughter Sarah and Piper J-3 Cub, Shelby, North Carolina, June 1963

Grob 102, after I spent the night in its cockpit, Luke Air Force Base No. 1, Arizona, June 1985

My son Adam and Beechcraft Bonanza, Socorro, New Mexico, 1978

With my wife Joanne and Mooney Mark 20, Boulder, Colorado, June 1970

My son Jason and Cessna 172, Orange County, California, 1970

Books by Kenneth Ford

The World of Elementary Particles

Basic Physics

Classical and Modern Physics (3 volumes)

Geons, Black Holes, and Quantum Foam: A Life in Physics
(with John Archibald Wheeler)

The Quantum World: Quantum Physics for Everyone

www.ianford.com/kenford
ken@hbarpress.com

Kenneth Ford

Ken with Crow Indian tie, 1999

enneth Ford has been a physics professor, a college president, an executive in a non-profit organization, a high-school teacher, a writer—and a pilot. Some of his previous books—all on physics—have made their way into seven languages. In 2006, he was recognized by the American Association of Physics Teachers with that organization's Oersted medal for contributions to teaching. This is his first venture into writing about his long-time passion, flying. He lives in Philadelphia with his wife Joanne. They have seven children and thirteen grandchildren.

Printed in the United States
142322LV00002B/75/A

9 780979 410413